SOCIAL STAKES OF PRIVATIZATIONS IN CAMEROON

SOCIAL STAKES OF PRIVATIZATIONS IN CAMEROON

Case of the Cameroon Development Corporation (CDC)

Hermann-Habib KIBANGOU

Translated by Goodwill Ghenghan

RESOURCE *Publications* • Eugene, Oregon

SOCIAL STAKES OF PRIVATIZATIONS IN CAMEROON
Case of the Cameroon Development Corporation (CDC)

Resource Publications
An Imprint of Wipf and Stock Publishers
199 W. 8th Ave., Suite 3
Eugene, OR 97401

www.wipfandstock.com

PAPERBACK ISBN: 978-1-5326-5983-6
HARDCOVER ISBN: 978-1-5326-5984-3
EBOOK ISBN: 978-1-5326-5985-0

Manufactured in the U.S.A.   06/25/19

From the same author

Enjeux sociaux des privatisations au Cameroun: le cas de la 'Cameroon Development Corporation' (CDC), Paris, Edilivre, 2009, 157 p.

La vision mvengienne de la paupérisation anthropologique. Une piste de réflexion philosophique sur le ntù? Paris, Edilivre, 2011, 112 p.

The Role of the Congolese Catholic Church in Promoting Social and Economic Justice in Relation to Oil, Outskirts Press, Inc., Denver, Colorado, 2011, 133 p.

Paulin Poucouta, Le service de la parole de Dieu. Entretiens, Editions Paulines, Abidjan, 2016, 168 p.

To my late Father Adolphe BOUEYE
and to my mother Cecile TSAKA,
I dedicate this piece of work.

Contents

Acknowledgements

To MY THESIS DIRECTOR, Dr Emmanuel WONYU who, by agreeing to supervise this end-of-cycle work, advised, helped and encouraged me till the end, I express my deep gratitude.

To Claude Ernest Kiamba, Firmin MBALLA, Constantin ABENA, Olivier IYEBI MANDJEK, Claude ABE, NKOULOU NKOULOU Zozo, Ludovic LADO, Serge Patrick BOUEYI, Roger Bertrand MOUANGA, Claude Martin DOMFANG, Herve LADO, ALANG Diane, I am grateful for comments and suggestions made. To my friends of Limbe and Kie Village, notably Brother Karl, Chief Ngambi, Mr. Fombe, Mr. Kamga, Mr. Obase, Mr. Moffa D. Mbongo, Cornelius Banah Sama, Mbongo's family, Chief Samson Motulu, I sincerely thank you.

To the Jesuit Communities of Yaoundé (Saint Francis Xaxier and Alberto Hurtado), friends and all those who, by their advice, made me think, I also say thank you.

Also, I thank all those who, from far or near, encouraged the publication of this piece of work: Kisito Matrengar Nantoiallah, Serge-Patrick BOUEYI, Michaelle Bidilou BOUEYI, Roland Brice-Ley KIZIBOUKOU, Raissa Cyrielle MAMPEMBE, Christelle Marina BOUEYI-TSAKA, Victoria RAVENTOS, Gervine Ngoma and Ghislain KORNA NOUDJALBAYE.

Acronyms and Abbreviations[1]

Blcc: Bakweri Land Claims Committee

Cdc: Cameroon Development Corporation

Cncr: National Council for Dialogue and Cooperation of Rural

Cstc: Trade Union Confederation of Cameroon Workers

Cte: Cameroon Tea Estates

Imf: International Monetary Fund

Minagri: Ministry of Agriculture

Minefi: Ministry of Economy and Finance

Sodecoton: Cotton Development Corporation

Sonacos: Senegal National Oilseed Marketing Company

1. This is selected at will.

General Introduction

FINDING

IN THE EARLY 60S, the independence of several french-speaking African states marks at the same time the first steps of the development of public enterprises[1]. New nation-states find themselves obliged to continue the work started by the former colonial powers to develop public services.

Several institutions for agricultural purpose are emerging, alongside the existing public services such as: water, electricity, public transport, savings-banks, municipal road commissions, etc.

A few years later, new nation-states decide to intervene directly in the most productive sectors of their individual economies. They are gradually replacing private contractors. This is the beginning of the nationalization policies. Among these policies, the most posted are "Maroquinisation", "Senegalisation" or even "Zaïrinisation". Thereafter, several companies such as banks, cement factory and other agro-industrial businesses are created or come under the direct control of the states, given the insignificant number of national private entrepreneurs valued without capital.

In the early 80s, the number of public or para-public enterprises is estimated at about 1,500 in french-speaking black Africa: 120 in Benin, 140 in Côte d'Ivoire, 180 in Senegal, 110 in Guinea

1. Chavane, Bruno. Bilan et perspectives des privatisations en Afrique francophone : une etape de la democratisation? http://www.abhatoo.net.ma/ maalama-textuelle/developpement-economique-et-social/developpement-social/etat-politique/privatisation/bilan-et-perspectives-des-privatisations-en-afrique-francophone-une-etape-de-la-democratisation.

1

and 115 in Cameroon. The State appears to be the only agent capable of developing the economy. Her intervention is deemed necessary. This is how countries like Cameroon, Côte d'Ivoire, Gabon or Togo advocate economic liberalism, while Congo, Guinea, Madagascar and Mali advocate planned economy.

In this environment where states are hostile to the private sector, the informal sector is growing, while the para-public sector continues to generate uneasy deficits. The low rates of economic growth, as well as those of population growth, characterize the 80s. The decline in purchasing power of the population increases unceasingly interventionism of States through public enterprises. In this light, state interventionism is increasingly challenged. The World Bank, the International Monetary Fund (IMF) and other international institutions, now apply their aid to the implementation of vigorous liberalization programmes. This is the beginning of Structural Adjustment Programmes and restructuring and reformation of public enterprises.

The devaluation of the CFA franc and the early 90s mark the second wave of privatizations recommended by international financial institutions. The transition from a system of *"social goals"* to that of private capital becomes more and more evident. From the peoples' point of view, the ongoing reforms imposed from outside, often do not take into account the specific situation of each country. Therefore, the question posed by privatization is: *how can a government conciliate the need to privatize a public company with that of the consideration of the claims of the people?* This is the fundamental question behind this thinking.

We chose as example the case of the *Cameroon Development Corporation* (Cdc). This is justified by the fact that, as announced, more than ten years earlier, privatization drags on, though it (Cdc) appears third on the list[2] of 15 public companies and parastatals to be privatized. After choosing to sell its four branches separately (banana, tea, rubber, palm oil), the cameroonian government succeeded in October 2002, to sell the tea industry to the south

---

2. Set by Article 1 of Decree No. 94–125 of July 1994

african group Brobon Finex, which created the Cameroon Tea Estates (Cte). This is, to date, the only branch privatized.

With its 13,000 employees, the first agro-industrial company in Cameroon, also first employer after the State, is a major stake. Also the planned dismantling raises much concern. As long as the state exploited the land and offered to local populations (Bakweri of the Southwest Cameroon) employment and social benefits at the same time, no problems arose. On the day of privatization, even if the land is just "granted" by a long lease (lasting up to ninety-nine years), local people are afraid to pay the price.

Thus, after the announcement of the decision to privatize the company in 1994, the aforementioned population, expressed concern about the fate of the land on which Cdc plantations are located which they claim as their ancestral lands, seeing with a dim view this land pass into the hands of a private company. Some of the elites of this community as well as traditional leaders of the said land organized themselves into the collective called Bakweri Land Claims Committee (Blcc). The Blcc leaders, who claim to be "accredited agents of Bakweri people", went up to the African Court on Human Rights for their rights to their ancestral land, according to them in their concession to the Cdc by the State meanwhile the said lands did not belong to her. They argue, in fact, that some 104,000 ha of land, on which Cdc plantations are since its inception in 1947, belong to indigenous Bakweri, who have occupied it since time immemorial. The State would have ensured the management, in confidence, on behalf of these people, who would have *agreed "against the grain"* to this arrangement in 1947, and would *"have not been consulted"* by the government to be aware of their intentions for the land.

The Blcc also states that the land in question, originally taken away from the Bakweri by the german colonial administration, was recovered later, when Germany lost the First World War and that these german private areas were declared *"enemy's property"* and placed under the custody of a custodian of enemy's property. In 1946, these areas of the enemy were declared *"redeemed"* by the british colonial administration and designated as *"Native lands"* to be held in trust for the Bakweri people. The land status was approved by a special resolution of the Trusteeship Council of the United Nations on "Bakweri Lands", adopted in March 1950.

These developments provide a legal base for claims by the Bakweri. Moreover, the Land Act of 1974 would strengthen the rights of claimants in that it classifies all *"recorded lands in the Grundbuch"*[3] this is the case of land leased to the Cdc—as *"land . . . subject to the right of private property."* In other words, these lands are not part of the national domain as defined in the Land Law.

The argument thus exposed seems very alluring. However, it evokes a sense of fear among the Bakweri and a disavowal of governmental project. Evidence of a misunderstanding with the authorities. Hence, a few questions: how can the cameroonian government dispel that fear and raise this misunderstanding? How can she continue her plan to privatize the Cdc, without alienating the social benefits of employees and the Bakweri ancestral lands? Ultimately, though, what should she do to reassure potential investors who do not appreciate the context of legal uncertainty?

The Scope and Purpose of the Study

Our study is in the field of Political Sociology which focuses, among others, on economic and social functions of political powers as well as social forces working with state policies and influencing their implementation. The point of interest in this field is that of inclusive state policies as: *"that, which public authorities do or do not do, and the reason why they do follow or not a particular course of action or inaction"* (Heidenheimer et alii.: 1978, cited in Durand and Weil 1997: 527). In these state policies, we focus specifically on privatization policies. To better understand the purpose of our study, clarification of concepts that structure our subject is required, namely "stakes", "social stakes", "public enterprise"and "privatization".

---

3. Cf. Republic Of Cameroon, Order n° 74–1 of 6th July 1974, on land tenure, Yaoundé, National Printing Office, p. 3.

Conceptual Clarification

In a broad sense, the concept of stakes refers to something that is at stake in a restricted sense; the term refers to something for which we fight for; something essential that is subject of covetousness. For example, a stake to power.

By "social stakes" we mean the Cdc as a social enterprise when it provides a source of living to its population on the one hand. On the other hand, the Cdc provides its employees with needed social services such as schools, clinics and housing. Therefore, it is difficult to impose such a task to a private buyer.

The concept of public enterprise refers to *"a company in which the public interest is at least 25% of social capital"*[4]. The concept of privatization that we borrow from the Presidential Order No. 90/004 of June 22nd 1990[5] is understood here as" *the process by which the State or a public or semi-public organization wholly or partially disengages to the benefit of enterprises regardless of their legal form (public institution, state company, mixed economy company or otherwise), in which she holds all or part of the capital.* "It is important to note that several authors have written about privatization.

Authors Talk of Privatization

There is an extensive literature on the issue of privatization, but few explicitly address the social stakes of these privatization policies.

Zaki Laïdi (1989: 278) make, for example, notice that:

> "Truly speaking, and beyond its economic justifications, privatization is the quintessential home of political passions. It therefore lends itself easily to manipulation of power and ideology. In most countries, it is not only to drag the centre of gravity owned by the public sector to the private sector, but to lay the rules of a new political and social order".

4. Republic of Cameroon, Decree n°86/656 of 03rd June 1986, article 2.

5. Republic of Cameroon, Order No. 90/004 of 22 June 1990, Article 1, paragraph 1.

For this author, privatization is the moment or never to lay the rules of a new social policy. In other words, it assumes a new strategy in the new context in which there are actors who implement these policies of privatization. With all that it entails as political passions and/or ideological passions or manipulation of power.
And Zaki Laïdi (1989: 278) to ask:

> "But why privatize? Should we see an effect of fashion launched by Mrs. Thatcher, the result of economic pressure of Western donors in search of lucrative operations for states, or a way out of the deadlock faced by the galloping nationalization? Probably all three, even if the last hypothesis is not the least important.

But at the same time, it seems very critical of the World Bank for example when he says that "the Bank (that is to say, the World Bank) walks in darkness. It finds daily the complexity of stakes of privatization and beyond economic liberalization. "Indeed, for Zaki Laïdi, privatization is at the same time an "effect of fashion"; the result of an "Economic pressure" on States by donors and a "Way out" of the deadlock faced by galloping nationalization. These three assumptions are actually present when we analyse the stakes of privatization policies. But it does not go without a number of difficulties in the very nature of such stakes. Those who are promoters believe they master these stakes, but once on the ground, they are disillusioned with the complexity of the privatization transaction. In this case, the World Bank. Which explains, among others, its path in darkness. This shows how privatization policies are one thing and their stakes are another.

In his article entitled "*Tango juridique sur les privatisations au Cameroun*", Maurice Kamto (2003: 298) makes notice that:

> "Like any strategic transaction, privatization cannot be mechanical. The set of interests that intersect and often clash imposes accelerations and slowdowns or downturns. By the way, as south american dancers, one takes a step forward and one can move back as much or more. Is awareness of its strategic stakes and socio-economic constraints that dictated to the cameroonian government

this kind of legal arabesques that are emerging on the privatization front in Cameroon?"

Awareness of the strategic and socio-economic stakes, make notice Maurice Kamto, make us think of this south american dance, tango, where dancers dependent on the situation and interests, impose strategies unto themselves. Privatization is not absent from this arabesque, insofar as you have to be clever and make in such a way that the opponent does not master from the very first step the strategy employed by he/she against whom he/she plays.

A little further, Maurice Kamto notes that in terms of privatization, Cameroon is *"a country where excessive sensitivity to the ethnic issue prompted them to seek regional balance or regional diversification even within private companies" (Kamto 2003: 308).*

Referring to the cancelled privatization of Sodecoton (Cotton Development Corporation), the author calls for vigilance in view of the strategic position of this company of Northern Cameroon. Because of the political and social sensitivity of the issue, this author also asserts that: *"this vigilance will be much needed in the privatization of the Cdc whose political and social sensitivity seems just as high, but for different reasons"*(Kamto 2003: 311).

For Maurice Kamto, one of the stakes of privatization policies is the excessive sensitivity of the ethnic question in these privatization policies. These are at the same time an opportunity to seek regional balance or regional diversification. The announced privatization of Sodecoton and its cancellation, show the extent to which politics is involved and how it manages the passions that arise on occasion. Because for the Cameroonian political authorities, trying to privatize Sodecoton is jeopardizing the control they have over the northern part of the country.

The situation of Sodecoton is similar to that of the Cdc, but the stakes are more or less different. And as for the land problem on which the Cdc operates, Maurice Kamto (2003: 311–312) writes:

> "Since the announcement of the decision to privatize the company in 1994, these people were worried about the fate of the land on which Cdc plantations are located

which they claim as their ancestral lands. Then quickly, some elites of this community and traditional leaders in the area organized themselves into a collective called Bakweri Land Claims Committee (Blcc) whose leaders claim to be 'accredited agents of the Bakweri people".

We, during our fieldwork, met Bakweri people who are riparian of the Cdc plantations in the Fako division. They clearly state that the land on which the Cdc is based, is their land, and at no price, would they accept to give up.

In *"Le Messager"*[6] no. 1526 of Monday, June 23rd, 2003, we read the following:

> "The quasi-judicial organ of the African Union, at the end of her 33rd session held in Niamey from 17th to 29th May (read 2003), in which she discussed, amongst others, the complaint of the Bakweri Land Claims Committee (Blcc) accusing the cameroonian government of violating their ancestral land rights on the Cdc land, an order directing to the Cameroon State, in the person of her leader, Paul Biya, to suspend the alleged alienation of the disputed land of the Cameroon Development Corporation (Cdc) in the Fako division, until the Commission rules on the merits of the dispute."

Also in *"Le Messager"*[7], we read:

> "The BLCC requests the African Commission to make recommendations to the cameroonian government, to affirm in writing that the lands occupied by the Cdc are private property (of Bakweri people) as defined in Chapter II of the Land Law of 1974; that Bakweri be fully involved in the negotiations for the privatization of the Cdc to ensure that their interests are effectively protected as a result of the privatization of the state enterprise; that the arrears of rent, due to Bakweri since 1947 for they have been expropriated without compensation, be paid to a Bakweri Land investment Fund in favour of the dispossessed natives; it should be allocated to Bakweri

6. Alex Azebaze, *"Le pouvoir intimide les Bakweri ;* "4 . . .

7. Alex Azebaze, *"Suspension possible de la privatisation de la Cdc ;* "4.

acting collectively in the shareholding percentage of each sector of the Cdc privatized, for example Cameroon Tea Estates; and finally, that the Blcc be represented in the current Board of Directors and future management teams as was the case under British colonization."

For his part, Jean-Marie Atangana Mebara (1997: 51), discusses issues of privatization policies, explicitly. In Chapter IV of his book, entitled *"Les enjeux de la privatisation des monopoles de service public au Cameroun"*, the question discussed is that of general and specific challenges. It is true that it is not about industrial and commercial companies like Cdc, but public service monopolies, we believe that there is way for companies other than public service monopolies. We are particularly interested in the general challenges to the extent that they are found in almost all privatizations. These general challenges are political, economic, financial, social and legal. On policy challenges, Jean-Marie Atangana Mebara notes that political challenges "can be enjoyed at two main levels: internally and in terms of foreign relations." We'll see how that reflects in the privatization of the Cdc.

The challenges of privatization are sources of debate by the various actors. As Abdelilah Hamdouch (1989:8) makes notice, *"political debates on nationalization and privatization [. . .] overshadow the substantive issues and mask the true economic and social challenges."*

As for Piet Konings (2003: 10), *"one of the privatizations in Cameroon that sparked off virulent opposition from ethno-regional associations and pressure groups was that of the Cameroon Development Corporation (Cdc), whose estates are located in the coastal area of Anglophone Cameroon".*

In this literature review, as well as our exploratory talks, we can remember that privatization is a controversial issue. Hardly, they were unanimous among the stakeholders, largely because they do not sufficiently take into account the social dimension and the process of transfer of state assets; it is characterized by a relatively high dose of opacity. This explains, in part, the doubts and concerns that many feed on it.

Problem Statement

Thus presented, our subject can be approached from several angles. Indeed, we can analyze it on the basis of "causes"(the question of *why*), "circumstances" (the question of *when*), the "manner" (the question of *how)* or "recipients"(the question of *in whose favour)* privatizations have taken place in Africa in general and Cameroon in particular. This type of questioning is common among non-specialists. It is also scrutinized by some experts in social sciences, because it offers the possibility of a comparative analysis. But, it easily lends itself to value judgments and makes easy the expression of a primary chauvinism in some people. So she would take us away from our project.

It could also deal with the privatization of the Cdc through the prism of the anglophone-francophone opposition. This reading, though shared by some of our respondents, would, more than any other, cantilevere with the goal we have set ourselves, namely: identify the "social stakes of the privatization of Cdc." Indeed, it would make us a prisoner of "passions" and "prejudices", forcing us to realize it, while taking side against our will.

One other possibility would be to study the various stakes of privatization policies. The subject is undoubtedly attractive, in view of the related exuberant literature. Only that, it would drag us to unknown places, unsuspected and certainly at odds with the question that underlies this analysis, because of the multitude of stakes.

All the approaches we just listed have in common the fact that they shunt our thinking on economic paths. However, in this process, it's not just the economic side. We might even say that there is a beam of aspects that are interacting. The success of this operation is measured, nowadays, on the ability of the government to take them all into account, and especially to consider the social dimension. For she is most likely to pose problems, as evidenced by the case of the difficult Cdc privatization. So then, *how to conciliate the profit with the social dimension of privatization? Specifically, with regard to the privatization of the Cdc, how*

can the cameroonian state continue the process of privatization, without giving away the social achievements of workers and lands of the indigenous, the Bakweri?
It is possible, from our point of view, to reconcile all of these concerns. Nevertheless, we should not lose sight of the fact that in such situations, stakeholders tend to maximize profit at the expense of others.

This problem statement has the advantage of reconciling social, political and economic policy-making. In addition, it takes us away from previous issues by exposing us as little as possible, the risks that we have previously discussed. Maurice Kamto and Piet Konings address the social stake more or less as we see it. The first, while alluding to the land problem, addresses the issue of privatization in a more legal context. The title of his article is very telling: *"Tango juridique sur les privatisations au Cameroun".* The second addresses the land issue from a perspective of social movement. We will abound in this direction, with greater emphasis on the sociological and anthropological dimensions.

Our Research Hypothesis

In order to answer our onset question *(how can a government conciliate the need to privatize a public company with that of the consideration of the claims of the people?)*, we formulate our hypothesis as follows, starting from the example of the Cdc: liberalization accompanying the privatization of the Cdc can undoubtedly be an opportunity to promote economic democracy, if it involves employers, workers, public authorities and indigenous populations in the search of appropriate strategies and methods.

Firstly, because the privatization of the Cdc is now presented as a major policy option that goes beyond the economic framework (secondary hypothesis 1);

Secondly, because the privatization of the Cdc will induce significant social impact on employment, the status of many workers, labour rights and the ancestral lands of indigenous people (secondary hypothesis 2).

11

We need to define this hypothesis through a number of indicators[8]:

- Renting of the land by the Cdc for a period of 60 years;
- The slow process of privatization of the Cdc since 1994;
- Recognition of these lands as part of the national domain or not;
- The appointment, these recent years, of prime ministers from the Southwest, particularly Bakweri;
- The social function performed by the Cdc, etc.

Regarding techniques of *data collection*, we initially chose literature research, namely: quantified and unquantified pre-set data. The quantified pre-set data are the official documents and / or records of the Cdc; statistics from other studies, etc. The unquantified pre-set data are literary works, biographies and life stories, advertising, etc. The literature research allowed us to do a close reading of the issues of privatization policies in Cameroon, specifically in the context of the Cdc. Secondly, we conducted sociological surveys by combining two approaches, namely the qualitative approach and quantitative approach. The quantitative approach allowed us to tackle our study from a questionnaire with the employees of the Cdc, the population of Limbe and the Bakweri. The qualitative approach allowed us to address the same study, this time with the executives of the Cdc.

Our study was conducted from March 21st to April 8th, 2005 in the city of Limbe (which harbours the social headquarters of the Cdc), specifically in the village inhabited by the Bakweri natives called Kie[9].

To construct our sample, we opted for the combination of random selection and choice-oriented. The process of choice-oriented was used in the questionnaire meant for workers of the Cdc as well as that addressed to Bakweri natives. All the inhabitants of

---

8. These easily observable indicators will allow us to test our hypotheses.

9. Read Kié.

Limbe had an equal chance to be part of the sample. It is with the latter category that the method of random selection is justified. The selected districts were Bota, Sokolo, Middle Farm, and New Town.

Cdc workers are actors at the heart of the stakes of privatization policies; therefore, they are involved in the process of rational choice, since they are active in the privatization process. Cdc workers selected for our survey are those who work at the Head Office in Bota and those of the Oil Palms Management Group (two structures in which we did our internship). Regarding Bakweri natives, we chose Kie village, because it is a village inhabited mostly by Bakweri natives.

Our sample consists of 114 respondents: 36 Bakweri (including a member of BLCC), 45 employees of the Cdc and 32 residents of Limbe. It is presented as follows:

Table 1: Overview of the sample

Places	Bota	Middle Farm	New Town	Sokolo	Kie village	Total
Respondents						
Workers of the Cdc	43	2	0	0	0	45
Inhabitants of . . .	10	4	15	3	0	32
Members of Blcc	0	0	0	0	1	1
Bakweri	0	0	0	0	36	36
Total	53	6	15	3	36	114

Source: Our survey data, 2005.

For the analysis model, we used the strategic approach of action systems as formulated by Michel Crozier and Erhard Friedberg, and the interactionist approach. For these two authors:

> "The interdependence of actors in the system appears to be reflected by the fact that no decision of any actor can be taken unilaterally: reaching an acceptable compromise is a prerequisite for any action (. . .) It does not

seem possible that a compromise be negotiated directly between the parties. Negotiation always seems to come about through the intervention of an instance of another nature "(M. Crozier and Erhard Friedberg 1977: 255).

The interactionist approach allows us to design politics like the plural act resulting in a set of contradictions, conflicts or coalition between different groups. These conflicts concern the official institutions and the entire periphery. This is the link to the heterogeneity of social relations, of "social pluralism" in the words of Robert Dahl and Linblom, (1954 Cited by Kiamba 2004-5) because power is characterized *here "by an unequal distribution of resources and positions of power between different actors in competition."* Applied to public policy, this approach induces a mode of thinking that considers the balance more or less stable between the groups as a factor. In addition, the content of public policies reflects all the rules born of momentary, ambiguous, lasting agreements between groups.

Some thinking patterns will enable us to better implement our methodological approaches. These patterns are: functional (nature of the phenomenon of privatization in its spatio-temporal context); actant (recognizing the intentionality of the action of the individual and the strategy he deploys as a rational calculation); causal (make the connection between cause and effect).

Our analysis of the social implications of the privatization of the Cdc is divided into two parts:

Part One: The Process Of Privatization Of The Cdc:
A Long Maturation.

Initially, we will convene the theoretical data of privatization. It involves analysing the data on a political, economic, financial or legal base that questioned the economic policy of the state and limit its interventions (Chapter 1). Then we will discuss the various steps involved in the process of privatization of the Cdc and seek to understand what blocks the said process (Chapter 2).

Part Two: A Privatization With Great Land Mustiness

This is about analysing the privatization of the Cdc from the perspective of the indigenous, that is the Bakweri, and from the perspective of allogenous mostly from Northwest Cameroon, nay even countries in the sub-region (Chapter 3). Then, we will analyze the official position which is that of the Cameroon State.

Our intention is to see how far and to what extent African states in general and the cameroonian State in particular, may accept the collaboration with representatives of the civil society in the game and the stakes of privatization policies, in the search for a social compromise.

PART ONE

The Privatization Process of the Cdc: a long maturation

THE CDC IS IN the process of privatization. The process ongoing, is especially complicated by the land problem with respect to plantations. If "the privatization process in Cameroon is always controversial as to its implementation, while it unleashes passions about the emotional impact due to companies subject to the process" (André Monkam and Joseph Nzomo 2002: 46.), that of the Cdc creates more controversy. So we wonder if the privatization of this agro-industry is a necessity or an international injunction.

In our study, it is important to consider first the reasons for privatization in Africa and Cameroon (Chapter 1). Then we will see in what the privatization of the Cdc is a clear requirement (Chapter 2).

Chapter 1

Reasons for Privatization in Africa and Cameroon

WHAT ARE THE OBJECTIVES of this chapter? We will identify the foundations of privatization in Africa; show that beyond a simple asset or business transfer, privatization affects the relationship between economic and social actors and between actors and the State. We describe the context of privatization of the Cdc while citing the political, economic, financial and legal foundations, just to name these few.

Several factors that we will analyze explain privatizations: political aspects (1), economic factors (2), the financial problem (3) and finally the legal issues (4). There is also the problem of the capital of public enterprises (5), as well as the land status of agro-industries (6).

POLITICAL ASPECTS:

" . . . It is not possible to understand the economic policies adopted in developing countries without involving the political dimension." (Jean-Dominique Lafaye, "La prise en compte de la dimension politique dans l'analyse economique" 2003: 213)

The political aspects will allow us to first identify the explanatory symptoms of State intervention in the sector of economy, and in another phase, the failure of the interventionist logic that led to the questioning of the action of the State.

Of what use are, we can ask ourselves, the descriptions of the State that we will summon? Indeed, we want to show the limits of the State; the fact that she is called upon to limit her interventions and hereby mark, the end of State interventionism and the beginning of her economic disengagement.

The relationship between these descriptions of the State and our study is more of a cause and effect, to the extent that one cannot talk of privatization without involving its historicity. The State, and therefore the policy, played a major role in the advent of economic liberalization.

The African State Indexed . . .

Abundant literature (e.g. Gaud 1967; Diakite 1986) exists on the role of African States in terms of economic and/or social regulation. Indeed, from independence until the 80s, a major fact characterized the State in Africa: the gradual extension of her grip on the economy. Phrases such as Protector-State, Providence-State nay even Master-State or Shareholder-State reveal this oversized role of the State. During this period, *State interventions were seen as the natural vector of economic 'take-off'*. (Jacquemot and Raffinot 1993: 15) Over time, specifically in the early 80s, this State interventionist policy will be ineffective, because of certain limitations. The State has failed in her mission to develop.

The State Has Failed . . .

The limits often identified for the failure of this State interventionism will come from Bretton Woods institutions (the World Bank and the IMF). Early critics they formulate against the States, back in the early 80s, after they have been consulted by the States who wanted financial assistance in solving their crisis. From that moment, the two institutions will, in addition to identifying the symptoms of State failure, denounce the various plans that made the State the sole instrument of development. Voluntary planning, like the exaggerated State control of the economy also explains the failure of the providence-State.

The Failure of the Providence-State

The providence-State is the characteristic of the African State in opposition to the recognition of the modern State by these four pillars: institutionalized power, administration, universalist laws and legitimized monopoly of coercion. In Africa, the providence-State has shown the absence of a real State in the modern sense of the term. However, all indications make believe that the State in Africa is still under construction. Understanding that State includes neo-patrimonial State qualifiers in connection with the crisis that will challenge the logic behind it.

The African State in Crisis

The management of the State was made in total ignorance of the needs of the community for the benefit of private interests, the State having proved unable to play her true role, for reasons ranging from overloading her outline.

The Overloaded State

This is the prototype of the State absorbed by all public offices, after the deconstruction by colonization of traditional social relations thereby fulfilling the social relationships that the State was supposed to do: education, health, food, etc. Accordingly, the State was overconsumed. Similarly, in the context of education, the effect of overload has been marked by the absorption of graduates into the teaching class. But in addition to being overloaded, the State was a predator state.

The Predator State

The other feature in the failure of the providence-State is her predatory management. A predator State is a State *"that feeds the company without giving it sufficient services to justify its existence.* (Jacquemot and Raffinot 1993: 24) Predation is characteristic of the use made of public property for personal use. In this sense, it goes beyond the framework of the State, and can both be used in settings such as limited government or public enterprises. In her predation, the State cannot make obey her laws; so it is a "slack-State".

The Slack-State

The providence-State is in the words of Gunnar Myrdal, a "slack-State" marked by non-compliance with rules issued by the authority, a secret agreement between the authority and pressure groups she is supposed to control, leakage of administrative control . . . not to mention the corruption and financial mismanagement. This will cause the Bank to make the following observation:

"The long list of development problems of African countries reflects crisis for power (. . .). Without a private sector sufficiently influential to curb their excesses, the servants of the State, in many African countries, served themselves without fear of being harassed (. . .). This resulted in a personalization of politics that forces politicians to develop customer service if they want to stay in power. Leaders arrogate wide discretionary powers and have no cure for legitimacy" (World bank cited in Jacquemot and Raffinot 1993: 26–27).

The socio-political analyses on Africa have in addition to defining the true nature of the State, identified the relationship between the State and civil society, between the confusion existing between public and private.

The Neo-patrimonial State

To understand this term, it must be made from the understanding of African traditional power as patriarchal power. This patriarchal power, closely based on kinship will mark the influence of the elder on his lineage. Thus, the patrimonial-State will expand this patriarchal power beyond the mere domestic setting. In this sense, the one that will exercise power will be surrounded by his family, his faithful servants and clients, without taking account of their competence or quality of the service they render to him. Only the duty and loyalty of members in respect of the head will count. Thus, the generous reward of docile members, and the rebuke of the less faithful. Clearly, patrimonial-State is managed in total confusion between personal business and those of the State. No clear distinction between public and private sectors. One of the thinkers of the patrimonial power is unquestionably Max Weber (1971) Jean-François Medard (1990: 28) is a contemporary author who has emerged in his writings on the patrimonial management of power in Africa.

Compared to patrimonial-State, the neo-patrimonial State refers to the post-colonial State, in addition to modern bureaucratic standards, making use of heritage standards. In other words, the "*neo-patrimonial management, that is to say, this particular way of articulating modern and traditional logic, has its specific institutions: one-party, centralized administration, mass organizations . . . often secured an ethnic base*"(Jacquemot and Raffinot 1993: 23). This can indeed lead to crisis, given the absence of established rules and standards.

Further analyses complement studies on the nature of the State in Africa. That of Jean-François Bayard (1989: 11–12) through the concept of "politics of the belly" has become a reference. Incidentally, he wrote the following:

> "The very phrase 'politics of the belly', is rich with multiple meanings that should not be ignored. It shows primarily situations of food shortage still prevalent in Africa. Eating frequently remains a problem, a difficulty,

23

a worry. Most often, however, the term 'eat' (pronounced in Cameroon with inimitable intonation!) denotes the desires and practices other than food. Above all, the accumulator activities, paving the way for social mobility and allowing the holder of power to be able to 'stand up'. [. . .] 'politics of the belly' is also that of banter, what Congolese call 'deuxième bureau [. . .] it is finally, in a more suspicious manner, the location of the invisible forces whose control is essential to the conquest and exercise of power: the eating can be symbolic and murders in the dramatic but daily form of witchcraft. Ultimately, 'politics of the belly' is a social phenomenon, as understood by Marcel Mauss.

After this entire list, to what form of government does Cameroon belong to? The State of Cameroon is a State under construction. Several aspects of the above descriptions are found in this country. Placing her in one of these descriptions give insufficient reading of the form of State to which Cameroon belongs. However, difficulties in the management of public enterprises may lead us to using concepts like "predation" or "neo-patrimonialism" in the cameroonian context.

In short, the urgent appeal of the World Bank will bring African States to revise downward their economic policies, and to end their interventionist logic. Hence, the transformation from a manager State to a guarantor State. But we might as well use the words "too much of a State" or "providence-State" to refer to the guarantor State, or "less of a State" to signify the end of State interventionism. This end will actually require a crisis. Hence, the importance of evoking especially economic data justifying the outbreak of the said crisis.

THE ECONOMIC FACTORS

The shift from manager-State to guarantor-State was not made unexpectedly. State operating enterprises having given disappointing results, became thereafter, deficient. For Cameroon, the crisis of 1986 will usher the unset of a new era.

The Crisis of 1986, an Important Interlude

The economic crisis of 1986 marks an important moment in the withdrawal of the cameroonian State from the economic sector, public companies haven shown their shortcomings. *"Public companies created, writes Touna Mama, have been disappointing; laxism of fiscal rules, the primacy given to political goals condemned them to gross inefficiency.*[1]

From that moment, Bretton Woods institutions will play a significant role in the economic life of Cameroon. This crisis will be costly to Cameroon who, after the oil boom from 1977 to 1985, will experience a period of turbulence. Already, between 1984/85 and 1987/88, the country witnesses the fall in international prices and the depreciation of the US dollar in FCFA, the consequence being reduced investments (Aerts and alii., 2000: 5).

Several factors explain the origin of this crisis: internal factors and external factors. But *"the origin of the crisis is to be found in external factors: downward adjustment in the price of oil and raw materials, particularly coffee, cocoa and cotton, but also change in the parity of the US dollar to CFA franc."* (Aerts and alii., 2000: 18)

The internal factors of the crisis have been masked by the possibilities offered by the oil windfall. Given the seriousness of the situation, a solution had to push to crisis that would only worsen (1985–1993).

For a Solution to the Crisis

The solution to the crisis is first of all economical.

> "Economists are largely interested in this issue of privatization, highlighting the various benefits that can be made in a country undergoing such a process. The main arguments seen in the basic books on the subject such as those of Bös (1991) and Vickers and Yarrow (1988), are organized around ideological and political reasons on the one hand, including a change in the distribution

1. Touna Mama, quoted by Abdul Bagui Kari, "Regard sur les privatisations ,"15.

of power in society and increased democratization and economic reasons on the other hand. In the latter case, the main justifications refer at the same time to the efficiency, the redistribution and the stabilisation."(Jellal and Wolff, 2003: 73–4)

In general, several authors believe that private companies are more efficient than public companies. The pronounced reason to this superiority is that, in the public sector, the cost of labour is relatively higher. However, lowering the cost of labour, we obtain an efficiency gain in the private sector. Thus, *"privatization of a public firm is assumed to increase the efficiency and productivity".* (Rees quoted in Jellak and Wolff 2003: 74).

In the same line, the argument refers to Leibenstein's x-efficiency theory. According to this theory, the internal environment as well as the external business environment is very important. In the external environment, Leibenstein thinks there is strong pressure on managers of public enterprises, which prevents these companies from being on their minimal cost curve. And the fact that employment contracts are written so evasive gives individuals some latitude. All this contributes to inefficient State enterprises (external environment). *"This is why Leibenstein thinks that the public company is generating X-inefficiency."*

Three factors explain this finding. The first factor shows how the public company *"operates in a protected economic environment, characterized by a near absence of competition."* The second factor insists on the fact that *"public companies often have a policy of favourable financing, allowing them to limit the probability of bankruptcy."* The third factor shows that *"public companies have multiple objectives, which are often incompatible with the requirements of economic efficiency and profit maximization."*

It is in these terms that one of the challenges of the crisis of the State was to restore a sound macroeconomic framework. But we cannot talk of economic data without referring to financial data.

THE WAY OUT OF A FINANCIAL PROBLEM

"Privatization has assured positive effect on public finances". (Jean-Marie Gankou and Dieudonné Bondoma Yokono 2003: 293). One of the financial stakes is probably *"the limited financial resources of all the organs that work on public funding so as to encourage them to resources of private financing"*. Another financial stake is the *"increase in financial contributions from consumers of public goods".* This in fact involves stabilization and fiscal consolidation.

Faced with the economic crisis in Cameroon, the State will be able to lower her expenses by implementing a policy of reform to which the IMF and the World Bank will provide support including rationalization of public expenditure and the restructuring of public enterprises.

"The process of enterprise reform, writes Abdul Bagui Kari,[2] took place in Cameroon in 3 different ways, namely: liquidation, rehabilitation and privatization; the choice of the formula is based on objectives and financial position of the company." The decisions taken by President Paul Biya being legally significant."

A LEGAL QUESTION?

In 1988, the President of the Republic of Cameroon sent a statement[3] to his ministers, secretaries of State and Board of chairs, guidelines on rehabilitation and restructuring of public enterprises and parastatals, asking them to:

"-Revise law on the orientation of business, taking into account two requirements, streamlining and progressive liberalization of distribution operations;

-Reduce as much as possible monopoly positions by encouraging the creation of competitive local exchange carriers;

---

2. Abdul Bagui Kari, "Regard sur les privatisations,"16.

3. See Instruction No. 007 / CAB / PR of 04th November 1988.

-Subordinate investments of public enterprises to prior achievement and systematic detailed feasibility studies to avoid waste of financial resources"[4]. Under Presidential Order No. 90/004 of 22nd June 1900,[5] in Article 3, (1) it is written that:

"Privatization operations can be performed as follows:

-by total or partial sale, to the private sector, of shares held by the State and public organizations in the enterprises to be privatized;

-total or partial sale, to the private sector, of assets of the companies to be privatized;

-getting into the capital of an enterprise of natural or legal entities of private law or their greater participation to the capital of this enterprise;

-lease or lease-management of assets and/or of funds of the company's business by natural or legal entities of private law;

-contract management of company with public participation by natural or legal entities of private law;

-any other recognized technical assignment.

(2) The transfer of assets under this section may be made in connection with the liquidation of a company or can be optionally followed by the dissolution and liquidation of the company."

4. Abdul Bagui Kari, "Regard sur les privatisations,"18.

5. This is by law n ° 89/030 of 29th December 1989 that the President of the Republic of Cameroon is authorized to lay down rules on privatization, by Order No. 90/ 004 of 22nd June 1990.

It is clear from this article that some flexibility exists as to the applicability of this or that privatization technique. Abdul Bagui Kari[6] specifies this well when he writes:

> "The Enforcement Decree No. 90/1257 of 30/08/90 in its Chapter I that covers items 1-6 lays down general provisions relating to the mode of privatization as specified in Article 3 of the Ordinance above-referred ; These modes are: direct sales, the increase in capital, concession, lease-management, merger or acquisition and any other valid means of income by law; As for provision relating to privatization techniques , cameroonian law drafted in general terms is flexible and allows the use of a range of techniques of equity as Specific needs of each particular case after evaluating the company to be privatized;

No legally binding technique is excluded."

Official institutions meant to implement these policies of privatization are: the Interdepartmental Committee of the mission. This is the decision making body. It is first composed of political and administrative authorities of the State and foremost is the Minister of Economy and Finance. The Technical Commission of Privatization and Liquidation is the technical body; it is under the supervision of the Minister of Economy and Finance.

The reform of public company poses, at the same time, the problem of transfer of their capital: a problem not easily solved, since it requires a careful review of the status of each company.

THE PROBLEM OF CAPITAL IN PUBLIC ENTERPRISES

Most public companies have, in the example of the Cdc, a capital from State coffers. With disappointing results from some of these companies, it is therefore difficult for the cameroonian State to continue maintaining them. In other words, the crisis of the providence-State is a questioning of the capital of public enterprises.

6. Abdul Bagui Kari, "Regard sur les privatisations, "21

To this issue of corporate capital, that of land status must be added. If the majority of companies do not have this problem, some do experience it as an obstacle. This is the case of agro-industries.

LAND STATUS OF AGRO-INDUSTRIES

In Cameroon, privatizations, while being the object of political passions, poses land problem to the State. The reaction that followed the announcement of the privatization of the Cdc is patent proof. Indeed, the legal uncertainty that exists around the land issue prior request expresses clarification of the cameroonian law. The land status of the Cdc, for example, highlights the colonial law (the time when the land belonging to the Bakweri was taken away), the right of independent Cameroon, not forgetting the 1994 cameroonian law announcing privatisations. (Kamto 2003: 311). According to the government's strategy for privatization of agro-industries, the land will not be sold, but given on a very long lease.

In this chapter, we have emphasized on the theoretical data which enabled African States in general and Cameroon in particular, to move from the logic of "too much of a State" to that of "less of a State". This analysis is, we think, essential to the extent that it shows us that reasons of various natures and often complementary form the basis of privatization policies.

The *"instrumental failure of the State"* a term we borrow from Jacquemot and Raffinot (1993: 15) is that of the master-State, owner of public enterprises. The State of Cameroon, to the extent where, to promote her development, explicitly intervened by injecting money in several public companies was also a master-State, given the investments made in the economy sector. In the words of Abdul Bagui Kari,[7] it was *"investments needed to promote and ensure economic growth assuming a huge financial mobilization that was not able to ensure national private operators."*

Evidence that the cameroonian government has not escaped this interventionist logic of master-State or shareholder-State is the creation of joint venture companies such as the Cameroon

---

7. Abdul Bagui Kari, "Regard sur les privatisations, "13.

Development Bank (Cdb) or the National Investment Company. However, it should be noted that State intervention was not limited to the economy; the social aspect was also taken into consideration.

Indeed, if the providence-State has her limitations, it is mainly because of the oversized role of manager-State, that is to say, a State whose function of management is more than rewarded . Beyond this overvaluation of the function of management, are the public companies that have come to be overvalued. In Cameroon, for example, *"in 1984, transfers and subsidies of public enterprises reached 150 billion CFA francs, that is 18% of public expenditure and 50% of oil revenue*[8]*".*

Far from working alone, the manager-State is driven by an ideological principle to a political, economic, social or administrative nature, which only reinforced her interventionism. Cases inherent to nationalism, socialism and communism, can indeed explain this political character. As for economic ideology, "Mercantilism" as well as "Keynesianism", may also be summoned. Administrative theory convenes, for its part, to developmental and evolutionary theses. Many African States have applied these theories believing to develop themselves at the same time. Unfortunately, the economic crisis that will hit public enterprises in 1980 will challenge the logic of the interventionist State. From that moment, the role of the State will be reduced, and lesser expression of manager-State will be used to benefit the guarantor-State now called to play a minimum role. Phrases such as the "minimum State" or "modest State (dear to Crozier) deeply express this State withdrawal from the economic sphere. The guarantor State is guided by the liberal economic ideology. One of the leaders of this current is no person other than Adam Smith who says the State should minimize her interventions. However, she can only act on issues related to national defence, public justice and peace, public infrastructures and public education. In the same line as Adam Smith, David Ricardo will insist on the minimum appropriate role of the State, particularly in terms of arbitration. This role of the

8. Abdul Bagui Kari, "Regard sur les privatisations, "14.

Cameroon State, among others, explains her decision to privatize the Cdc.

Chapter 2

The privatization of the Cdc: an Ambiguous Requirement

OUR INTENTION IN THIS second chapter is to present the Cdc from its configuration (1); to retrace the steps of the process of privatization (2). Then, we will describe the perceptions of employees and local people (3). Finally, we "will say" something on the privatization of other companies (4).

STRUCTURE OF THE CAMEROON DEVELOPMENT CORPORATION (CDC)

Created on January 1st, 1947 with a surface area of over 42,000 hectares, about 100,000 allocated to the Cameroon government, the Cdc is a development company[1] with active capital 15,626,328,000 F CFA. 100% owned by the cameroonian government, it is the oldest and largest agro-business company in Cameroon, and the largest employer after the Cameroon government, with an estimated staff of 13,000 workers.

Indeed, the Cdc was created to acquire, develop and operate large plantations of tropical crops such as hevea (rubber), palm oil, palm kernel, coconut, black pepper, banana, and formerly tea. It is present in 4 of the 10 Provinces (Kibangou 2003: 3) of Cameroon:

---

1. See Decree No. 82/038 of 22nd January 1982.

- In the southwest, in Limbe (Fako division), in Kumba (Mémé division), in Mundemba (Ndian division)
- In the northwest, in Nkambe (Donga Mantung division)
- In the Littoral, in Nkongsamba (Mungo division)
- In the west, precisely in Dschang (Menoua division)".

The Cdc has already been reorganized in September 1973 and January 1982. Since its inception, it has had three development programmes:

- The Camdev I (1967–1974)) [2]
- The Camdev II (1978–1987)
- The Camdev III (1987–1997)

At its inception, it was called "Cameroons [3]development Corporation" and not "Cameroon Development Corporation." The difference here is simply the letter "s" (from Cameroons) that differentiates the first name from the second. The elision of the letter was in 1972, after the unification of the country. And when the British government decided to create this business, it was in order to *"manage and develop all german industrial plantations expropriated in 1939"* (Courade 1975: 128).

Initially, the Cdc had its headquarters in Onika (Lagos), Nigeria. F.E.V. Smith was the Board Chairman. A year later, the Head Office was transferred to Bota (Limbe). In 1951, began the construction of the current Middle Farm complex, still in Limbe, with a Hall, schools and shops. In 1997, the Cdc celebrated its 50

---

2. Camdev, means Cameroon Development. These are extension programmes of the Cdc (implementing agency), permitting expansion of her plantations of palm oil, hevea, etc.

3. It should be said that the Cdc has had a name change quite striking in its history. Reading the report of 1959, we realize that it was called 'Colonial Development Corporation' before 'Cameroons Development Corporation. See Colonial Development Corporation (Cdc), Report and Accounts 1959 Annual Report Statement of Accounts for the year to 31 December 1959.

years of existence. When I did my internship in 2003, it was in its 58th year of existence.

The General Management was ensured by Mr. Henry Njalla Quan [4]. In office since 1997, succeeding the former Prime Minister Mr. Peter Mafany Musonge. The General Manager is in fact appointed by the President of the Republic. Mr. Henry Njalla Quan was the 3rd Cameroonian [5] at this position, and the 11th General Manager since the creation of the Cdc in 1947. The first 8 General Managers haven been British.

The General Management is assisted by four departments: the department of finance, the department of human resources, the department of information technology and the department of inspection and controls. At the Cdc, all the departments have the same status. And work is so decentralized that they work hand in glove. However, each department is centralized into administrative, agricultural, and support structures.

Administrative structures include:

- Services directly related to the supervision of the General Manager. Their mission is to coordinate action plans and projects across the enterprise.

- The department of Human Resources whose mission is to identify needs in terms of manpower, updating training or formation of staff.

- The financial department that handles accounts of the company. It is divided into three services which are: accounting, treasury and payroll.

- The Information Technology department is responsible for the creation and maintenance of softwares.

---

4. Note that he and his predecessor are native Bakweri. "Franklin Ngoni Ikome Njie, was appointed GM of Cdc by Presidential degree No. 2012/631 of Wednesday 19th December 2012 following the death of the late GM, Henry Njalla Quan on 13th December 2012.

5. The first was John Ngu Niba and the second Peter Mafany Musonge.

Agricultural structures are now 3 in number: rubber, palm oil and banana. These structures are responsible for the production, both in terms of quantity and quality. They should set the price of products, taking into account production costs, and are dedicated to customer satisfaction.

Support structures have some inherent role to ensure the goal of each department for technical and social conditions. For example:

- The technical services department whose mission is to ensure the functioning of electricity, the condition of vehicles and electronic devices;

- The transportation group that handles everything related to transportation;

- The procurement department that takes care of equipping the company with necessary materials and tools;

- The commercial department which handles local and export sales.

Under the supervision of the Ministries of Agriculture (Minagri) and Finance (Minefi), the Cdc in addition to the General Manager , includes a Deputy General Manager, an Executive Board of 12 members representing all the various ministries and some parastatal companies.

Staff at the Cdc is represented by staff representatives and unions. There are, for example trade unions like the Farmers Union; the Fawu (Agricultural Workers Union); Agricultural Confederation of Cameroon; Kupe Muanenguba Workers Trade Union; the Departmental Trade Union of workers of Agriculture, Fisheries and Livestock of Mungo; Trade Union Confederation of Workers of Cameroon (Cstc). The Fawu plays a key role since the announcement of the privatization of the Cdc.

The Cdc is working with several organizations, which from the outside, participate in the perpetuation of the corporation. We can mention: Agrisol and Del Monte Fresh Produce.

Customers are of three (3) types: retailers (are smaller clients, mostly individuals), wholesalers (often corporations such as limited liability companies, profit-making companies), and finally industrialists. Regarding specific products, they are unwrought, semi-finished or finished.

THE CDC, AS SEEN BY ITS EMPLOYEES AND "CUSTOMERS"

The image that people have of the Cdc depends on several factors, as they participate in productivity, buy or consume its products.

We asked our respondents what the Cdc represents to them. Here is what they told us:

Table 2: Perception of the Cdc by the inhabitants of Limbe by level of study

N°	What Cdc represents is:	Primary	Secondary	University	Percentages	Total
1	Employment to many Cameroonians	0	5	0	14	5
2	A simple state owned corporation	0	2	1	9	3
3	The largest corporation in Cameroon and the second employer after the government	2	3	6	31	11
4	Industrial exploitation of banana, rubber, palm oil, etc.	0	9	4	37	13

	Other answers		2	1	9	3
			2	21	12	100	35

Source: Our survey data, 2005.

14 percent of respondents agree that the Cdc employs many Cameroonians, which is not wrong especially as it employs thousands of people.

9 percent think the Cdc is just a simple State property. This statement is not false because the Cdc is owned by the cameroonian government.

31 percent believe that the Cdc is the largest corporation and the second largest employer after the government. Cdc employs 13,000 people. In this sense, this response goes back to the first; which would give 45 percent of respondents who think that the Cdc is the largest company in Cameroon. This is very important for our analysis because we focused our study on the social dimension of privatization.

However, 37 percent "only" identify the Cdc in the industrial production of banana, hevea (rubber), and palm oil. When found in this region, one is indeed impressed by the visibility of these rubber , banana, and palm oil plantations.

However, what image do Cdc workers have of their company? To this question, we collected the following answers.

Table 3: Perception of the Cdc by its workers

N°	What Cdc represents for you ?	Primary	Secondary	University	Total	Percentages

1	The biggest agro-in-dustrial corpora-tion in Camer-oon			15	15	33
2	The second em-ployer after the state		13		13	29
3	Our work life for many years		7		7	16
4	Employ-ment in S-W province	10			10	22
					45	100

Source: our survey data, 2005.

33 percent of workers in the Cdc say bluntly that their company is the largest agro-industrial corporation in Cameroon. In dialogue with certain employees of the Cdc, we read on their face, a kind of pride for them to work in the largest agro-business company of Cameroon.

29 percent believe that it is the second largest employer after the government. This response brings us more or less to the first. This means that 62 percent of respondents share the same view.

16 percent think that the Cdc represents their work since many years. This portion of the respondents is that which has rich experience in terms of seniority and held in conjunction with a cutting position on the privatization of the Cdc.

22 percent believe that the Cdc represents employment in the South-West province. Here, it reflects as in the previous table, the social dimension of the Cdc. The Cdc must indeed be looked upon as a whole, with all that it entails as health, sports, education facilities, etc. As for health infrastructure, it has two hospitals (Tiko and Mukonje), 20 developed health centres, clinics and health stations. According to the 1999[6] statistics, 15,986 employees and 23,762 family members received health care. Here lies the true social function of the company.

The data collected in the field allow us to better understand the reaction of the people of the South-West and even the North-west, with the announcement of the privatization of the Cdc.

ANNOUNCEMENT OF A CHANGE

The privatization of the Cdc is fixed on July 14th, 1994 by Article 1 of Decree No. 94–125. Among the 15 companies to be privatized, it appears (already mentioned) third. The cameroonian State has opted for privatization by sector, only the tea industry had been privatized since 2002. Since then, the Cdc following its privatization process, which process is defined as *"a set of provisions of any kind made by State authorities to devote the policy of total or partial withdrawal of the public body to the private sector and all other operations that were conducted as part of this policy[7]"*. One step in this process is probably the call for competition.

The Call for Competition

To guarantee the transparency of any privatization operation, and make a sale that takes into account public interest, the shift to the call for competition seems necessary. This is manifested by calls for tender by the State. With regard to the Cdc, prequalification of international opinions were launched in December 1998.

6. Cameroon Development Corporation, Annual Report and Accounts for the Year ended 30th June1999, 35.

7. Abdul Bagui Kari, "Regard sur les privatisations," 18.

Another call for tender to study the modalities of privatization was launched. Scrutiny done, the "Cooper & Lybrand's" cabinet was selected to conduct the study and submit a report before June 30th 1998[8]. If the report was made, it remains that the privatization process still follows its course. The call for tender of 1998 having failed, another was launched in 2000 and led to the sale of the tea industry. As for other sectors, *on the basis of a new strategy, the government initiated the updating of strategic studies. These studies are ongoing. The timetable adopted plans to launch the tender by early 2005*[9]. So far, nothing at least officially, is said about this tender.

We meant above that, the announcement of the privatization of the Cdc provoked the reaction of the Bakweri, which more or less hinders the privatization process.

Why is the Privatization of the Cdc Hindered?

In the words of Maurice Kamto (2003: 311), "the process of the privatization of this company has been very slow due to the reaction of the Bakweri of Southwest Cameroon, riparians of the Cdc plantations."[10]

Given that several companies were to be privatized, it seems necessary to know those that were and those that were not. This allows us to know if the obstruction experienced by the Cdc is a problem particular to this company.

References to the Privatization of Other Companies

Alluding to other companies, we aren't moving any inch away from our subject. We seek to understand why other companies didn't experience the same blocking as the Cdc.

---

8. Cameroon Development Corporation, Annual Report and Accounts for the Year ended 30th June 1999 Limbe, Presbyterian , 11.

9. See website: http://www.ctpl.cm/prog_en_cours/agro_in_cdc.htm

10. We will return to this issue further in the second part of our study, with data we have collected on site during our investigations.

In fact, since the cameroonian government decided to privatize public and parapublic enterprises,[11] many of these companies have either been removed from the list, privatized or liquidated nay even liquidated and privatized at the same time, or privatization being in course or at the stage of preliminary studies[12].

The Sector of Agro-business in Cameroon

The agro-food sector in Cameroon is not highly competitive. As proof, there is on the national scene a few companies that are on the farm. For example some companies that have had to be privatized. This is for example the Society of Banana plantations of Mbome ex Ocb (Banana Marketing Board sold to the fruit Company, a French private group, at 2 billion 281 million CFA francs on December 20th 1990[13]) and the Cameroon sugar company (Camsuco). The latter had as activity, the production of sugar cane, with a capital of 1.3 billion CFA francs of which 98.12% owned by the State.

> "The financial tenders, recorded, writes Abdul Bagui Kari,[14] were those of the American group Vilgrain (Somdiaa-Sosucam) for eleven (11) billion FCFA; Castel for four (4) billion and SUGAR Bank group for four point seven (4.7) billion.
>
> Sosucam controlled by Somdiaa (Vilgrain group) is the new owner of Camsuco and now controls the sugar industry in Cameroon. It has spent 11 billion FCFA in favour of the state and is committed to invest over $ 21 billion; land is leased by the State."

11. See Decree No. 90/1423 of 3rd October 1990.

12. See Jean-Marie Dieudonné and Gankou Bondoma, "Les privatisations dans le processus d'ajustement structurel au Cameroun."In Bekolo-Ebe et al., 295–6.

13. Abdul Bagui Kari, "Regard sur les privatisations,"32.

14. Abdul Bagui Kari, "Regard sur les privatisations,"31.

There is also Socapalm (Cameroon Society of palm plantations), founded in 1968 and sold in December 1997 at 18,450,000,000 CFA francs. 100 percent owned by the Cameroon State (as the Cdc), the company is in oilseeds. On this day, its capital is divided between: Palcam/Cogepart Group, 60 percent that is to say 28 percent to Monthe group (Sofincom) and 28 percent to Socfinco and finally 4 percent to donors; other private investments, 27 percent Cameroon State, 10 percent and ultimately the staff, 3 percent.

Then comes the Spfs (Society of Palm plantations of the Switzerland Firm) Palmor, purchased by Siph (International Society of Hevea Plantations), a Malaysian operator. 92 percent of the capital is owned by the Frabinvest/Bakou group and the rest goes to the state. The Oncpb (National Development Board for Poultry and Small Livestock) was purchased at 120 million FCFA by Cameroonian investors. To this list, we can add the Society of hevea in Cameroon (Hevecam). Our interest is not only limited to the agro-industrial sector.

We can see, privatization of these enterprises in the agro-industrial sector did not pose as many problems as the announced privatization of the Cdc. The specificity of this company can be linked to its "social enterprise" character.

Other Sectors:

Among the companies listed, there is for example the National Printing Office (In); it remains unique because to the best of our knowledge, it is the only company to have been removed from the list.

There are also companies that were liquidated. This is the case of the General Metal Works (Getram), the Development Corporation of Plain Rice Mbo (Soderim), Society of Shrimp Cameroon (Crevecam), the Equipment Company for Africa (Seac), the Studies Society for the Development of Africa (Seda), the Cameroon

Society of Tourism (Socatour), the Cameroon Society of Tobacco (Tbs), the Urban Transport Company of Cameroon (Sotuc), and finally the Pharmaceutical National Board of Cameroon (Onapharm).

As already privatized enterprises, we mention: the editing and production centre for teaching and research (Cepec), Cameroon Metallurgical Society (Scdm), the Chocolate factory Cameroon (Chococam), the Lumberyards Operating Company Cameroon (Sepbc) sold at 1 812 millions,[15] Cameroon's Society of handling and stevedoring (Socamac), the Coastal Refining Company (Srl), the National Board of Railway Cameroon (Regifercam), Cameroon Shipping Lines (Camship), the National Electricity Company of Cameroon (Sonel), Cameroon Telecommunications (Camtel), Cameroon Telecommunications-Mobile (Camtel-Mobile), the National Park of Engineering Equipment (Matgenie), the International Bank of Cameroon for Savings and Loans (Bicec), the Insurance Company of Cameroon (Socar).

In the same time, Ceper did yield to the cameroonian government 500 million of FCFA. It was bought by Mutual professionals Education of Cameroon. Chococam on its part yielded 200 million FCFA. The Scdm 300 million FCFA, and Socamac 850 million FCFA.

Other companies were simply liquidated and privatized at the same time: the Forest Society Belabo (Sofibel), the Plywood of Cameroon (Cocam). There are also companies with preliminary studies are underway: the case of Cameroon Airlines (Camair). There is a company on the list of companies to be privatized, of which the operation was never initiated. This is the case of the Camtainer.

Among the companies with privatization is underway, we mention: the National Water Company of Cameroon (Snec), the Cement Industry Cameroon (Cimencam), the Cameroon Oil Storage Company (Scdp), the Cotton Development Corporation

15. For other businesses, read Abdul Bagui Kari, "Regard sur les privatizations," 32.

(Sodecoton) and ultimately the Cameroon Development Corporation (Cdc).

To sum it all, we note that the cameroonian government attaches significant importance to the operation known as transfer. According to Daniel Potash, the most convenient option is sale or gratuitous transfer. If the author prefers the transfer or sale as a form of privatization, still it is a form of privatization amidst many. The table below gives a brief overview.

Table 4: Forms of Privatization

Delegation	Contract	for part of the service
		on comprehensive management
		by the concession of contract
	Concession	by renting
	Grant	
	Good supply	
	Mandate	
Divestment	Sale	to a joint venture
	Gratuitous transfer	to a private buyer
		to the public
		to employees
		to users or consumers
		to a joint venture
		to the public
		employees
		users or consumers
		the original owner (restitution)
		to selected recipients
Substitution	Liquidation	
	Deficiency	
	Withdrawal (dropping a charge)	
	Deregulation	

We specifically inserted this table insofar as during our surveys, our respondents were asked to give their views on privatization, the ideas they have vis-a-vis economic policy.

Among the companies cited above, many have not been a major problem for their privatization. However, the situation of Sodecoton poses as many problems as that of the Cdc.

The Case Study of Sodecoton: More Specific Than That of the Cdc?

In terms of turnover, Sodecoton is the first agro-business in Cameroon. Indeed, *"the cotton industry occupies an important place in the economy. It allowed the modernization of the countryside of Sodecoton while achieving outstanding performance in terms of yield (1500–2000 kg / ha). Presently, more than two million people live on this culture in the three northern provinces*[16]*"*.

Privatization of Sodecoton poses as many problems as that of the Cdc. Each company provides an intensive and superior labour compared to other companies. Cdc because it is the largest employer after the government, and Sodecoton because it feeds more than 2 million people. In either case, the regional sensitivity as well as the political sensitivity cannot go unnoticed. After the failure of the first attempt to privatize Sodecoton, the record was a big delay. Seven years after the launching of the call for tender in 1997, differences of opinion exist as to the form of privatization of the company.

If the case of Sodecoton is as specific as that of the Cdc, the fact remains that privatizations in Cameroon are still valid. From the North to the South-West, local people generally understand the meaning of privatizations.

Interviewing residents of Limbe, we obtained the following answers to the meaning they give to privatization.

Table 5: Opinions of Limbe inhabitants on privatization

16. See http: //www.cm/prog_en_cours/agro_in_coton.htm

N°	Meanings of Privatisation	Primary	Secondary	University	Total	Percentages
1	The sale of state own enterprises to private entities for better management		10	5	15	43
2	Taking over government enterprises by private individuals or sectors	1	14	2	17	49
3	Bad experience			2	2	6
4	Nothing	1			1	3
		2	24	9	35	100

Source: Our survey data, 2005.

It is clear from the table that 43% of respondents see privatization as the sale of State-owned enterprises to private entrepreneurs for better management. While 49 percent believe that privatization is the taking of government-owned enterprises by given individuals or private sectors. 6 percent agree that privatization is a bad experience, while for the remaining 3 percent, it means nothing.

Our purpose is not to determine whether privatization is good or bad, but to analyze the consideration of the interests of people in public policy, the data above show that the phenomenon of privatization is more or less understood by our respondents according to their level of study.

In the same view, Cdc workers as stakeholders in the privatization, did not hesitate to give us their thoughts on privatization in general. This approach we made, had a handicap: the question on privatization we earlier provided in our questionnaire, was removed for the simple reason that it is prohibited at the top hierarchy of the Cdc, to approach the problem of privatization without being expressly authorized by the Directorate. Obviously, only the General Manager can broach the subject. Consequently, we were forced to remove from the questionnaire, questions that were related to privatization which might disrupt our investigations. We, during our stay in Limbe, asked to meet the "GM", but unfortunately he was traveling. We wrote to ask him to grant us an interview on it. We are still waiting for his response.

However, against all odds, a fact, however, surprised us. It is this "*asymmetry in information*"[17] that we found even within the Cdc company. In the sense that only the General Manager or his closest associates know when and how the privatization of the Cdc will proceed. The workers know that their company will be privatized, but they ignore the time and how the said privatization will happen. Certainly, the Directorate feared the reaction of the workers which may result in internal tension within the company and create the effect known as "*moral hazard*"[18] by workers who, for example, could take action that will harm the Directorate of the Cdc.

However, we used to talk "*unofficially*" of this problem with the workers of the Cdc (in the premises or outside the premises of the company) so they could give us their opinions. Not surprisingly, they made known that they did not want the Cdc to be privatized. Here are the responses we received.

Table 6: Opinions of CDC workers on privatization

N°	Do you want CDC to be privatized?	Total	Percentages
1	No, we (workers) don't need privatization. Why is the government so determined? Even all the population is against privatization	25	56
2	No, I don't want to talk about it	12	27

17. There is information asymmetry when the parties signing an agreement do not have the same access to information. This is the case between the leadership of the Cdc and its employees.

18. A situation in which the signer of a contract may take actions that will harm the other part. That can simultaneously cause the effect known as "adverse selection"because the hirer has more information than the other party about his situation; so he can use it to take advantage of the contract.

3	We have no choice	8	18
4	Yes, we want it	0	0
		45	100

Source: Our survey data, 2005.

Data in this table reflect that Cdc workers in no way want their company to be privatized. All those we interviewed have outlined this. Of the 45 workers, no one was in favour of privatization. As against 56 percent who are annoyed to see that the government is determined to go ahead, then they say that all workers, including the people of Fako, are quite against the idea of privatizing the Cdc; 27 percent say they do not want to broach the subject, either by fear of being caught talking about it, or because they do not want to hear; 18 percent say they have no choice, because the position of the government will triumph, as the Cdc is a public company.

These data reflect the complexity of the phenomenon of privatization. It must be understood in the background with the privatization of the tea sector, and all the consequences it has caused. During our investigations, we went to "Tole"[19] a town located a few miles from Buea. We were impressed by the dilapidated premises where the tea manufacturing plant is. "Lifeless" houses reflected the sadness of employees. A situation, say certain employees of the CDC, they had not known before the privatization of the tea sector. Indeed, for problems such as health, workers could easily get

19. Read Tolé..

to the Cdc clinic and pay 300FCFA[20] as consultation fee. Today, all these benefits are non-existent.

We also collected the impressions of native Bakweri on their idea of privatization. We will come back to the Bakweri when it comes to addressing the land issue. For now, we stick to their views on privatization. The observation that we make on their position is really no different from the position of the Blcc; which is also not surprising.

Table 7: Opinions of Bakweri on privatization of enterprises in Cameroon.

N°	What do you think of privatization?	Total	Percentages
1	In our situation, we accept privatization if land problems are taken into consideration	17	46
2	Privatization must consider the people's will	13	35
3	Privatization depends on the sector	7	19
		37	100

Source: our survey data, 2005.

46 percent of respondents, from this table, affirm that we should talk of privatization if the land issue is taken into consideration;

however, 35 percent think that privatization should consider the will of the people;

for the remaining 19 percent , that depends on the sector to be privatized.

Here we must take into account that the Bakweri natives are not so much against the idea of privatization. They just want us to take into consideration their claims even before the privatization of the Cdc. Clearly, they want the issue of land devolution to be settled, that is to say, their lands be returned and they themselves be involved in the process of privatization. This is where we think is at stake in their claims. The fact that 46 percent relate privatization to land is indicative of the situation in which most Bakweri

20. Less than 1 USD.

are. It is not surprising that privatization may make them think about the issue of land. Presumably, they are affected by this issue. Indeed, one of the key stakes in privatization policies can be reduced to the influences that form around. There is, in fact, no privatization for privatization. These influences have an effect and logic. By evoking them, we do not shy away from our subject, but we apprehend more the phenomenon of privatization in relation to the social question. The positions of actors changing according to their logic and influences received.

According to Savas (2000), many influences are involved in privatization policies.

Table 8: The influences in favour of privatization

INFLUENCE	EFFECT	LOGIC
PRAGMATIC	Better government	Prudent privatization Leads to more productive public services
ECONOMIC	Less dependence on government	Growing prosperity allows more people to provide for their own needs, making them more receptive to privatization.
IDEOLOGICAL	Less from the government	Government is too big, too powerful, it mixes too much of people's lives and therefore it is a danger to democracy. Policy choices of the government are by definition less worthy of trust than the market. Privatization reduces the role of government.
MERCANTILE	More business opportunity	Government expenditure held an important place in the economy; could and should be in a direct larger share to private companies. The companies and the means of production owned by the government could be better utilized by the private sector.

POPULIST	A better society	Individuals should have more choices in terms of public services. They should be able to define and meet their common needs, and create a sense of community addressing less to distant administrative structures and their families, their neighbourhood, their church, their ethnic and humanitarian associations

Source: E.S. Savas 2000: 7.

Taking into account the social issue of privatization should enable African governments in general and Cameroon in particular, to be more "realistic" in their choices. Implying caution in the definitions of public policy, and therefore privatization.

Through privatization policies, reflect a complex logic, of which the stakes do not appear clearly at first sight. From the look of things just on the economic side, the analysis of these stakes becomes inadequate ipso facto. When added to the political side, the analysis becomes a little more balanced. In the sense that the stakes of privatization policies, beyond economic reasons that a State can set ahead, is a field where political passions are most clearly expressed. That's what we noticed with Bakweri land claims. Thus, it is not enough to privatize a company, it is still necessary to consider its history and culture of its milieu of existence. The case of the Cdc is itself probably a specificity related to its "social function", dating back over 70 years. The proof is that many companies whose privatization was announced at the same time as the Cdc, are now privatized, and because their social function appears "minimal" compared to that of the Cdc.

After this first part entitled "The privatization process of the Cdc: a long maturation", it should be noted that with the phenomenon of globalization, we are seeing more and more of such cases where States decide to privatize companies without taking into consideration the views of the people, or even predict their responses. It is as if it were enough to decide on a privatization that things happen. This way of looking at privatization policies shows a lack of analysis of the social dimension of the problem. In deciding to privatize the Cdc, the cameroonian authorities did not anticipate the long-term consequences of such a decision. In most cases, decisions are made without adequate field study.

"*As it should be very simple, writes Patrick Sandouly* (2005: 55), from a comfortable western capital office, to draw a line under the history and culture of a company. And to decide on behalf of profitability, globalization, or any other reason economically wise, it has to leave the bosom of the State to go private".

Examples abound on the continent. And the agricultural sector does not withdraw from this analysis. In Abdoulaye Wade's Senegal for example, there is the National Counsel for Consultation and Cooperation between Rural (Cncr) which asked the government of this country, to "break" the privatization of Sonacos (National Marketing Company of oilseeds Senegal). If it does not exist here, or at least there is no mention of land claims, it must be noted however, that there is a similarity between Sonacos of Senegal and the Cdc in Cameroon. The privatization of the two companies was announced some ten years. If Sonacos eventually ended being privatized since April 7th, 2003, the Cdc is not yet, although many sources say it will be by the end of 2005. In 2018, the Cdc is not yet privatized.

In addition, the agricultural sector is the base of livelihoods in Africa for several thousands of people. In Senegal, the peanut sector alone sustains some 4 million farmers. In Cameroon, the Cdc sustains 13,000 families. In Mali, one might add, the Malian Textile Development Company (Cmdt) which feeds more than three million Malians. Though the latter (Cmdt), as well as Sodecoton in Cameroon, are on the list of enterprises to be privatized. Our States should increasingly consider social reactions that mark the existence of a deep social malaise.

PART TWO

A Privatization with Great Land Must-

iness

WE WILL IN THIS second and final part of our study, analyse the reactions of the indigenous and the allogenous (Chapter 3), before trying to understand the reaction of the Cameroon State vis-a-vis the Bakweri land claims (Chapter 4). It means for us to analyze the discourse on the privatization of the Cdc and local realities.

Chapter 3

The Privatization of the Cdc: Views of Local People

IDENTIFY PERCEPTIONS OF THE privatization of the Cdc by the indigenous and allogenous and show shifts between the plans of the State and the reality as experienced by the people, are the objectives of this chapter.

This chapter has four parts. The first will allow us situate our investigation scenes so as to make of it place names (1). The second part will lead us to understand the position of the Bakweri as indigenous (2), while the third part will lead us to understand that of the Blcc (3). We will finish this chapter with the position of Northwest nationals also called "grassfields"(3).

A LOOK AT THE INVESTIGATION SCENE

This is as we announced earlier, Limbe and Kie village.

Limbe

Originally, Limbe was called Victoria, referring to "Queen Victoria" from England. In 1858, the city saw its first missionary post installed, by Alfred Saker, who called it as such, Victoria. *"It is, writes George Courade (1975:88), to the spanish government of Fernando*

Poo deciding to chase the Baptist missionaries that Victoria owes its creation".

Victoria became Limbe by Presidential Decree on May 16th 1982. Then, where did the name Limbe come from? During our research, we went to the Limbe Provincial Library. In reading, we came across a magazine published by the Limbe municipality. We learned the hard way that the name Limbe comes from the Limbe River, named after an engineer called Limburgh.

We can read the following: *"The new name (Limbe) was derived from the river that runs through the city (Limbe River), which also acquired its name from one engineer, Limburgh who constructed the first bridge at the entrance into the town.*[1]*"*

The city of Limbe is the capital of Fako division; it has a sea port and seaside resort on the Atlantic Ocean, and is located, by road, 75 km from Douala the economic capital, 350 km from Yaounde the political capital, 985 km from Ngaoundere, 310 Km from Bafoussam, 170 Km from Edea, etc. You can see from Limbe, the mountain that bears the name of the country, huge ovoid volcano (which is shaped like an egg) with an altitude of 4,070 metres. Decorated with a botanical garden of about 1,500 trees tight against each other, Limbe is in addition to its black sand beaches, (Mile 8, Mile 11 and Mile 6) a great point of attraction for tourists who come on weekends, mainly from Douala, doubtless because of its proximity.

Kie Village

Kie village is a village mainly inhabited by native Bakweri. Certainly, none Bakweri are present, but they are very few. Originally, the name of this village was Ekie-Kie, which means *"they have refused a place".* They, are the Bakweri,. In other words, the Bakweri refused because of the hill (Bakwerians refused because of the hill). Kie is populated by more than 150 people.

1. Limbe Municipality, 2.

An Opening to the Atlantic Ocean

The town of Limbe, in addition to its wooded hills, is surrounded by the Atlantic Ocean. If we look at the green gold in this study, the presence of oil because of the ocean, is not negligible at all. Indeed, thanks to the Atlantic Ocean, Cameroon has a major oil company, Sonara. Through its capital, the National Refining Company is of greater stand than the Cdc. "But green gold is nothing compared to black gold that gives Limbe the identity of oil capital. The city harbours the national Refining Company (Sonara), flagship of Cameroon mining. Sonara serves as growth engine to Limbe.[2]"

The presence of the Cdc in Fako division is of paramount importance. The majority of the population of this division thrives on agriculture. What do we retain from the Bakweri or indigenous people of Fako?

THE BAKWERI, A PEOPLE AT THE MARGIN OR AT THE BORDER?

> "It's a problem of truth about the nature of membership in a social group. We must begin by saying that xeno-phobia is natural and spontaneous. It must be admitted, and the question is what you make of it, not denying it (Paul Ricoeur, quoted by Dominique NGOIE-Ngalla, Le retour des ethnies. Quel Etat pour l'Afrique? (2003: 99).

According to Prince Ayuk A. Kima and Daniel Lyonga Matute (1990: 17), all the people of Fako division, thus the Bakweri, speak Bantu languages, a language group that one might find in Kenya, Congo, Uganda and South Africa. *"All the people of Fako Division, they write, nevertheless speak languages of Bantu family a linguistic group which could be traced across Kenya, Congo, Uganda and South Africa."*

Originally, indeed, Fako was the name the natives used when talking of Mount Cameroon. This is the name that was later used

---

2. Jeune Afrique Economique. Special Edition. Cameroun cap sur l'an 2000, 240.

to refer to the whole division. But we can only understand who the Bakweri are if one goes back to their history. Here, the use of social history can be of great use.

Typology of the Bakweri People

Typology of peoples (Séverin Cécile Abega 2004) , allows us to distinguish them from each other. Thus, we have for example shifting hierarchy of peoples (the principle of hierarchy moves depending on circumstances), as is the case of Aka, Baka or Bakola. Peoples flexible hierarchy, like the people of the forest, the Beti, the Fong, the Douala or Maka. Peoples high hierarchy: the case of the Bamoun, the Tikar, etc.

It turns out that during our investigations, we discovered that the Bakweri people are of flexible hierarchy; they are sedentary. Those we met at "Kie village" have a leader in the person of Chief Samson Sama Motulu. Each village has its head, so to speak. If Bakweri say they are Bantu, what do others say about them?

The Bakweri Seen by Others

We, in the course of our investigations, asked our respondents to tell us what they know of the Bakweri. This is for example the inhabitants of Limbe or better still Cdc workers. Here are the answers we gathered:

Table 9: Opinions of Limbe people on the Bakweri

N°	Responses	Frequency	Percentages
1	Bakwerians are very good people although they gossip a lot.	1	3
2	Bakwerians are people who are located at the coast of Cameroon. They have solely transformed the CDC to their own personal corporation	1	3
3	Bakwerians are lovers of luxury.	3	9
4	Bakwerians are inhabitants of Fako Division	11	31
5	Nothing	4	11
6	No answer	2	6

7	Bakwerians are the people who have most of the momentous occupation in Cameroon like delegates, ministers, etc.	1	3
8	Bakwerians love white-collar jobs. Are lazy. Love selling lands.	9	26
9	Bakwerians are self- centred and do not think about future. For them "it is always the present".	1	3
10	Bakwerians are those who fought the Germans in the late 1800	2	6
		35	100

Source: our survey data, 2005.

The table above shows how opinions are given in a spontaneous and diverse manner, as to the question of who are the Bakweri.

Obviously, 6 percent of respondents claim that Bakweri are those who fought with the Germans. This response should be taken into account insofar as it reinforces the view that considers the Bakweri as native Fako; in other words, they are in this division, the first to have met the Germans.

3 percent say Bakweri are egocentric people who do not think about the future. This point held by a minority deserves some attention for what is to follow.

6 percent say Bakweri are lazy people who only like to work in offices, like to sell land and do not like to do dirty jobs such as working with machinery. The expression "*White-collar jobs*" is very significant here. This view is also advanced by Georges Courade (a French geographer) in the analysis he made on the Bakweri people.

3 percent of respondents say that Bakweri are those that have the largest number of personalities in the country, following the example of government delegates, ministers, etc. This statement is exaggerated though partly true when you consider

the current prime minister and his predecessor who are both native Bakweri[3].

6 percent give no answer, while 11 percent say they know nothing about the Bakweri. Yet 31 percent say that the Bakweri are native Fako, while 9 percent say they like luxury.

On the remaining 6 percent , 3 percent say Bakweri are good, even if they like to talk too much; the other 3 percent say Bakweri are located on the coast and they have transformed the Cdc into their own heritage; this is not true. The most shared view is that which recognizes the Bakweri as originating from Fako. This confirms the idea that, in this division, they were the first to oppose the privatization of the Cdc. Therefore, it is difficult for the government to continue the process of privatization of Cdc, without alienating social achievements of workers on the one hand, and indigenous land on the other hand. The latter, in spite of what they have experienced since colonial times are, we can say, in search of their identity.

The Bakweri in Search of Their Identity

"The more nature is generous, writes Jean-Paul Ngoup-ande (1994: 45), and abundant, the lesser man tends to make an effort. [. . .] The abundant and generous nature does not grow in the effort, forecasting, planning and economics".

The fact that the Bakweri are blessed by nature, would it justify their lazy attitude? Indeed, they assert they themselves that when one is at Mount Cameroon, one can find everything to eat, provided one doesn't take anything alongside. We also sought the views of workers from the Cdc, about what they think of the Bakweri:

3. In 2003.

Table 10: Opinions of Cdc workers on the Bakweri

N°	Responses	Frequency	Percentages
1	Bakwerians are a tribe around Mount Fako area	10	22
2	Bakwerians are the natives of Fako Division	8	18
3	Bakwerians are cordial people	5	11
4	Bakwerians are the landowners of Fako Division	22	49

Source: our survey data, 2005.

Of the Cdc workers interviewed, 22 percent said that the Bakweri are a tribe living around Mount Cameroon; 18 percent say they are natives of Fako division, while 11 percent say they are friendly, and the remaining 49 percent say they are landowners of Fako division. These views do not differ much from those put forward by the people of Limbe.

According to the french geographer Georges Courade[4] the Bakweri people are a population dominated by the Third World. As he wrote in substance:

"The study of a society dominated by the Third World in terms of Group Policy seemed more fruitful in terms of the Bakweri people. The state of marginality, he said, in which it sinks is the result of its inability to regain its living space looted by the German colonial power, safeguard its true identity towards immigrants and a distant and centralized State and stay in power after having voted at the granting of independence by the British. It is proper to stop the hesitant approach of the group both in its demographic as well as socio-political behaviour so as to seize the share of non-reducible free-referee".

When, in fact, we came up with our problem statement, it was actually to understand the reaction of the Bakweri as a "community." And as Georges Courade specifies: "This is, in fact, studying a company in its relations with the colonial or central government

4. Georges Courade, "Marginalitee volontaire ou impose? Le cas des Bakweri du mont Cameroun, "357–88.

whose rigorous struggle resulted in the maintenance of this popula-tion at a distance, at the margin as far as land, economic and socio-political aspects are concerned. "It is only from this context that we can understand her position in line with the privatization of the Cdc.

The historical and socio-political context made the Bakweri to withdraw unto themselves. This is neither a leak nor any quest for a lost paradise, much less a proud rejection of modernity and so-called consumer society, thinks Georges Courade. For the lat-ter, in fact, *"we are dealing with a marginalized population who cannot narrate unto themselves, a form of collective suicide that may be similar to that of Native Americans after the Spanish conquest. "*

According to Georges Courade:

> "The Bakweri people, in fact, were a privileged witness, a remarkable indicator of what was the colonial impact, participation in the commercial economy and nation-building in one of the State's most fragmented Black Africa, who was found in spite of herself, sometimes in the first few rows at the drama and heartbreak experi-enced by the Anglophone Cameroon since the German conquest of 1884".

Today, more than ever, the Bakweri people remain this "privi-leged witness," this "remarkable indicator" since the announce-ment of the privatization of the Cdc. In this sense, it appears as one of the social actors that the cameroonian government cannot do without, not to talk of history. Indeed, when allusion is made in the first contact in between the Bakweri and Germans, the first thing that catches the attention of casual observers, is this vio-lence including decision by force to take the land belonging to the Bakweri by german settlers. An inhabitant (Mola Ndeley Mokoso 2000: 31–32) of Limbe speaks of this encounter as follows:

> "Liengu-Mboke and Fo are the Bakweri names for New Town and respectively. The present New Town was a forest until a group of sixty Bakweri led by their lead-ers Peter Mokoko Mokeba first chief of Liengu- Mboke and Nanjia settled on the present site. They had hitherto

occupied the area around the present Botanical Gardens and the old Basel Mission Church. It is said that the Germans ordered the natives to leave, as they later did with other villages in Fako to make room for their residential areas and plantations".

The analysis of land as a major stake to the privatization of the Cdc should indeed back from the german colonial period since it is at this point that the problem came to being and hitherto has not found solution. The authorities in Yaounde, are they as ready to find a solution to this problem? This question deserves indeed to be asked.

This long development on the Bakweri is essential to understand our problem statement to the extent that, the cameroonian government cannot continue the process of privatization of the Cdc while ignoring the indigenous people. These are indeed a key partner in the pursuit of the privatization process. But what are the relationships that the Bakweri have with the government of Cameroon?

The Bakweri we interviewed say they have good relations with the cameroonian government. This statement is astonishing when you consider the land issue which is at the origin of their claims but understandable when you consider that some Bakweri people occupy special places in government.

Table 11: Type of relationship between the Bakweri and the government

Responses	Frequency	Percentages
Our relationship with the government is:		
Fine	3	8
Fair	10	28
Fairly good	2	6
Other reasons: the appointment of Bakwerian prime ministers	21	58
	36	100

Source: our survey data, 2005.

These data are indicative of views often interested of native Bakweri, and strategic of the government.

8 percent of our respondents say they have a good relationship with the government;

28 percent believe that their relationships with the government are reasonable. This percentage reached the foregoing insofar put together (36 percent), they refer to the same reality qualifying relations of harmony that the Bakweri believe to have with the government of Cameroon;

6 percent say they have good-shaped relationships;

58 percent gave reasons that are more political by claiming that they are in the government (having a prime minister, a Bakweri, in the person of Mr. Ephraim Inoni); others come up more and more with the land issue, meaning that it is the only problem they have with the government. In evoking the land issue, it is necessary here to refer to this Bakweri organisation, the Blcc, which intends to negotiate with the government to address the land used by the Cdc.

Thus, this way of perceiving the government by the Bakweri imaginary refers to a word that we have shown in the table below:

Table 12: Perception of the word government in Bakweri language.

Language	Expression in Bakweri language	Literal translation
Bakweri	Likanaya	government

Source: our survey data, 2005.

Relations of Bakweri and "likanaya" (government) are centred more around the vision of the Blcc. We'll see why.

FROM BLC TO BLCC: BETWEEN MEMORY AND PRESENT

Indeed, historical differences exist in between Blc and Blcc. But in reality, it is the same committee.

The Blc (Bakweri Land Committee): the Memory

The Bakweri Land Committee predates the Blcc (Bakweri Land Claims Committee). Indeed, the Blc has existed since 1946 and oversees the monitoring of land tenure problem that Cdc operates on. As specified by Georges Courade: "... *The Bakweri had constituted a Bakweri Land Committee (1946) to recover their land.*" Coming to talk of it, Piet Konings wrote:

> "As soon as the privatization of the Cdc was announced, the Bakweri chiefs and elite mobilised to revive the moribund BLC and to adopt a common position with regard to the privatization, which had been planned without any consideration having been given to the Bakweri land problem. Soon thereafter, the Blc was renamed the Bakweri Land Claims Committee (Blcc)."

The Blcc (Bakweri Land Claims Committee): the Present

One cannot truly understand the reaction of the Blcc only if one refers to its context. In other words, it is only from this context that we can understand the logic of its action.

"*This Blcc, writes Maurice Kamto (2003: 312), whose representatives would have been received by the Representative of the government for the first time in December 2000* [5] argue that some 104,000 ha of land on which Cdc plantations are since its inception in 1947 belong to indigenous Bakweri who have occupied it since time immemorial, the State having assured the management, trust, on behalf of these populations. These private lands have been leased, according to the Blcc, to the Cdc for a period of 60 years until 2007 by their owners, Bakweri, who consented 'against the grain' to this arrangement in 1947, and 'were not consulted 'by the Government to take notice of their intentions regarding these lands".

---

5. 6 years after the announcement of the privatization of the CDC.

The Blcc in Action: the Pursuit of a Motive!

Blcc initially contacted the cameroonian government, in order to secure a successful outcome to the land problem. This approach by the Blcc went wrong for the simple reason that the government did not want to tackle this problem. Accordingly, the Blcc appealed to the African Commission on Human Rights. Since then, it continued with a mobilization and information campaign to keep the international community informed of the situation.

The efforts of the Blcc can be considered a historical action insofar as it is a set of activities that does not only provoke, but also intensify or slow the transformation of the social organization either wholly or partly (See Alain Touraine 1999 or Guy Rocher 1968).

In 2003, for example, two delegations from the Blcc respectively made a trip to Niamey (Niger) and another to Banjul (Gambia). In its letter of February 22nd 2004, the Blcc wrote:

"Ever since the Blcc started its international campaign for the restoration of Bakweri ancestral land rights before the judicial panel of the African Commission on Human & Peoples' Rights, two major delegations were dispatched last year to plead the Blcc case before the African Commission.

The first delegation of five Travelled to Niamey, republic of Niger, where Blcc was awarded an Injunction Against the Government of Cameroon, restraining her from further Top alienation of Cdc disputed lands, until the matter before the Commission is finally determined. The African Commission clearly Understood the gravity of the Bakweri complaint. On returning to Cameroon, BLCC again pleaded with Government to initiate negotiations for amicable settlement of the dispute, but there has been no reaction, as hitherto, to this request. The second delegation of six persons went to Banjul, Gambia, only last November, where both parties to the dispute made oral presentations in support of their respective written pleadings. As the Blcc matter has caught the eye of the International Community, the University of Tennessee, USA, sent to Banjul an attorney from its legal clinic, to lend backing to Blcc's lead counsel's submissions."[6]

The action of the Blcc took a magnitude that exceeds the borders of Cameroon. In a letter dated June 16th 2000 addressed to Mr. Horst Köhler (Manager of the IMF), the Committee wrote:

"The Bakweri, speaking through the Bakweri Land Claims Committee in the USA (Blcc-Usa) hereby reiterate their unwavering opposition to-any privatization program that does not take into consideration the legitimate rights of the natives whose ancestral lands are soon to be privatized Cdc which its colonial predecessors have exploited without compensation for more than a century".

Such a determination gives to think, that a public policy that does not take into account the needs of people will struggle to advance, to the extent that the deep malaise that causes its decision disappears with great difficulty. To date, in fact, the Bakweri are moved by this experience. By asking them about the ownership of lands operated by the Cdc, we collected the following data:

Table 13: Opinions of Bakweri over lands used by the Cdc

N°	Responses	Frequency	Percentages
1	We are the landowners of the land on which CDC operates	36	100
2	We are sure	36	100
		36	100

Source: our survey data, 2005.

6. Mola Njoh Litumbe, Secretary-General, Bakweri Land Claims Committee (Incorporated Registered as 01 in the Companies Registry, Limbe). P o Box 124 Buea, Cameroon.

Not surprisingly, the Bakweri we interviewed stated that they undoubtedly are the owners of the lands used by the Cdc and that they are sure.

Wanting to understand the perception and the meaning they have of land, we had this as information.

Table 14: Perception of land by the Bakweri

Language	Expression in Bakweri language	Literal translation
Bakweri	Monyè	Native land or ancestral land

Source: our survey data, 2005.

In Bakweri language, the term "Monyè" expresses both the birthplace and ancestral land.

According to Maurice *Kamto (2003: 311) "the privatization of the Cdc is a more complex problem combining land status of plantations to be privatized, colonial law and law of independent Cameroon and Cameroonians since 1994".*

Thus, based on colonial law, solving this problem is a delicate issue (See Stanislas Melone 1972). Indeed, legal uncertainty remains around the land problem. There is no evidence to date, at least materially, to an agreement that was signed between the german settlers and the Bakweri. The latter, through their collective support adamant that the Cdc has leased their land for a period of 60 years, so therefore it was in 2007 that ends this renting. This echoes the assertion of Piet Konings (2003: 16) when he writes: *"it pointed out that the Bakweri had never been paid royalties for the use of their lands since the establishment of the Cdc in 1946 and also stressed that the Bakweri were not inclined to renew the 60-year Cdc lease, thus reclaiming the Cdc lands after its expiry in 2007."*

The Bakweri have made their claims to the government of Cameroon. According to them, the latter did not listen. Otherwise why haven filed a complaint against that government to the Commission of the African Union on Human Rights?

According to the proposal of the Commission, the Cameroon State by her President, *"should make every effort to ensure the protection of ancestral rights of the Bakweri on their lands in the privatization of CdC"* (Alex Gustave Azebase 2003: 4). According to officials of the BLCC some of which claim to have received death threats or intimidation, the injunction was not well received by authorities in Yaounde.

Through this panel, we want to affirm the idea of a particular approach to the land problem with native Bakweri. It is an approach that emphasizes the view of Bakweri actors: the strategic analysis. In other words, we focus on the relations of Bakweri men and women with respect to land, and their different ways of accessing land. Through their land claims, the Bakweri want to show that *"the control of land and resources is (and most especially) a stake to power"* (Philippe Lavigne Delville 1998: 261).

> "As part of the concessions granted to settlers or to private companies, protection of 'rights of the indigenous' remain formal and is more of the Administration's worry to control customary initiatives or the living conditions of family or village communities." (E. Le Bris et alii., 1982: 20).

Ideas are worthy but by their arguments. As for reasons advanced by native Bakweri , we collected the following:

Table 15: Reasons advanced by the Bakweri on land ownership

N°	Responses	Frequency	Percentages
1	The land was owned by our forefathers who were asked to leave by the area by the Germans	27	75
2	We gave CDC the land. CDC never bought the land from us; the land is our ancestral heritage	5	14
3	The land was given to CDC for rent for 60 years	1	3
4	The whole of Fako Division was first founded by the Bakwerians	1	3
5	Other reasons (see map)	2	5
		36	100

Source: our survey data, 2005.

From this table, it appears that 75 percent of respondents say that the land of Fako division on which the Cdc is installed belonged to their ancestors to whom the Germans had asked to leave. 14 percent say that the land was given to the Cdc, and that the latter had never bought the land which is their ancestral heritage. 3 percent say that the land was leased to the Cdc for a period of 60 years. 3 percent say the whole Fako was founded by Bakweri. Finally 5 percent think it is enough to see the map of Fako.

The struggle of the Bakweri people is of many decades-old, this did not stop the privatization of the tea sector.

Note on the Privatization of the Tea Sector

It would indeed not be wrong to raise the problem of stopping the process of privatization of the Cdc specifically citing the case of the tea sector. Blcc members challenged the sale of the tea sector because it was done without solving the problem of land devolution. These members, while warning the executive chairman of Brobon Finex, Derrick C. Garvie against *"false declarations"* of the minister of Finance at the time, Mr. Meva'a Meboutou, who claimed that the land occupied by tea plantations is *"state property,"* say that, *"the rights of native Bakweri on Tole/Bwiyuku lands are intangible".*

In the sale of the tea sector made to the South African company Brobon Finex PTY Limited on October 18th 2002, the State (sole shareholder of the Cdc) sold 65% of her shares to the Cte. According to the press,[7] all a blur remains about the true nature of the South African company. The Blcc believes that the privatization of the tea sector wasn't transparent. Hence, its letter to the government to cancel the said privatization *"Bakweri tell government to revoke privatization of Cdc tea estates."*[8] The government's response was not long since President Paul Biya ordered investigation on the disputed purchase of Tole, Ndu and Djutitsa plantations. All this confirms the questioning inherent in the purchase of the tea sector. Namely: the redemption price decreased from 3.191 to 1.5

---

7. See for example, The Herald, June 22–23, 2003.
8. See for example, The Herald, June 22–23, 2003.

billion; the questionable source of funds; the questionable legal status of the major shareholder Brobon Finex, etc.

Social stakes of privatization of the Cdc are not only felt by the natives. Northwest nationals are deeply involved in this crisis.

INTERVENTION OF THE NORTHWEST ALLOGENOUS

In Fako division, privatization of the Cdc, far from interesting only the native Bakweri, involves people of the Northwest, also called "grassfields." Not only are they the most important labour force of the Cdc, but also because the Cdc is present in the Northwest, specifically Nkambe (Donga Mantung division).

This Common cause that the Bakweri and "grassfields" share, trump indeed internal problems between the two communities[9]. In so doing, they form a kind of regional coalition. In this effect, Piet Konings[10] wrote: "*In addition to the anglophone and South associations, there were other organisations in the region that resisted the privatization of the Cdc. The most significant was the Fako Agricultural Workers 'Union (Fawu) that is responsible for the representation and defence of the Cdc workers' interests.*"

It is not surprising that the Fawu as a union of farmers, be actively involved in these claims. But to show the regional aspect of these claims, as we can cite other associations, in addition to the Blcc: the Southern Cameroons National Council (Scnc), the South West Elite Association (Swela), the South West Chiefs' Conference (Swecc), etc.

And Piet Konings continues: "*Following the government announcement of the CDC privatization on 15th July 1994, all existing ethno-regional associations and opposition parties rallied to form a united front to resist government's decision.*"

This coalition around the privatization of the Cdc also shows a recognition of Bakweri as the owners of the land on which this company operates in the Fako division.

9. Piet Konings, "Mobility and exclusion," 169–94.
10. Piet Konings, "Privatization and ethno-regional protest," 14.

The data gathered explain this recognition. Asking indeed our investigators if they had ever heard of Blcc, the following answers were given to us:

Table 16: Opinions of Limbe inhabitants by level of study on Blcc

N°	Have you heard about Blcc?	Pri-mary	Second-ary	Univer-sity	Total	Percentages
1	Yes	1	15	9	25	71
2	No	0	8	2	10	29
3	No answer	0	0	0	0	0
		1	23	11	35	100

Source: Our survey data, 2005.

It is clear from this table that 71 percent of respondents say they have heard of BLCC; while 29 percent say the opposite. This shows that the Blcc is not unknown.

In the same line, here are the views of workers of the Cdc interviewed on the Blcc:

Table 17: Opinions of Cdc workers on Blcc

N°	Have you heard about Blcc?	Frequency	Percentages
1	Yes	45	100
2	No	0	0
3	No answer	0	0
		45	100

Source: our survey data, 2005.

All employees of the Cdc affirm to have heard of the Blcc. This shows that privatization of this company is of great social sensitivity, and presumably, employees of the Cdc couldn't haven't heard of the Bakweri Land Claims Committee.

On the question of who are the landowners of the land on which the Cdc operates, this is what our respondents say:

Table 18: Opinions of Limbe inhabitants on the owners of Fako lands

N°	The owners of the land on which CDC operates	Primary	Secondary	University	Total	Percentages
1	Bakwerians	2	14	10	26	74
2	Government		3	1	4	11
3	CDC		1		1	3
4	No answer		1		1	3
5	I don't know		1	2	3	9
		2	20	13	35	100

Source: Our survey data, 2005.

74 percent of respondents say that it is the Bakweri who own the land on which the Cdc operates;

11 percent say it is the government that owns the land; 3 percent claim that it is the Cdc;

3 percent give no answer, and finally 9 percent say they do not know.

All employees of the Cdc we interviewed said they at least heard of Blcc, even if they do not know this structure from top to bottom. This statement does not surprise us that in Fako division, it is the Bakweri who are indigenous. Moreover Cdc workers originating from Fako, shall inform anyone who wants to listen, that it is their ancestors who had agreed that the Cdc be installed where it is now.

We must not lose sight that the reaction of Bakweri must be seen in its original context, that, they react according to a problem of development they are facing, precisely because of a government decision they do not just appreciate the procedure, for the simple reason that they were not involved in this decision.

"The problem of development, writes the Congolese historian Dominique Ngoïe-Ngalla (2003: 117-118) , that is usually placed under the economic aspect only, but that should be asked in a comprehensive manner, taking into account the whole man, biological being, reasonable being, spiritual being, is basically a problem of maturity, of the level of consciousness, of awareness by the individual of the need to fight to emerge from the cave."

It is necessary and urgent to even think that the problem of development should allow both our States and our ethnic groups to see together in the same direction, to build the national edifice. *Because "only the participation of all ethnic groups in the formulation of decisions of the State common citizen, could save Africa from ethnic endemic disorder and mal- development which, constantly contradict predictions of policies and projections of economists."*(Dominique Ngoïe-Ngalla (2003: 131–132).

Chapter 4

The Cameroonian Government at the Bar

WE WILL GO INTO this final chapter to highlight cameroonian legislation on land; present the reactions of the cameroonian government over Bakweri claims; and highlight the ways out of the crisis.

Looking at things closely, it is difficult to talk about official position of the Cameroon State. Instead, rather mutism seems to reign. Where does this mutism come from? We think it's necessary to convene first of all the cameroonian law (1). Then, we can discuss the reaction of the State, better that which seems to be a response to the Bakweri (2). We will end our analysis by inquiring into the possibility of resolving the land issue of the Cdc. Under these conditions, how can we hope to achieve a social compromise? (3).

AROUND THE LAW IN FORCE

Under Ordinance No. 74-1 of 6th July 1974 establishing land regime,[1] in its article II, it is stated that: *"Are subject to private property law; lands listed below:*

a) registered lands;

1. Republic Of Cameroon, land and federal regime. Land tenure and state lands, 3.

b) freehold lands;

c) land acquired under the transcript regime;

d) final frontier concessions;

e) lands recorded in 'Grundbuch.'

In this case, the lands claimed by the Bakweri belong to the last category, *"the lands recorded in Grundbuch."* In this sense, they are lands not belonging to the national domain.

> "If the disputed land, asks Maurice Kamto (2003: 312), are likely to have the status of private property, have they ever been turned into private property in accordance with the current legislation on land? And for whose benefit? Bakweri community or a few individuals? Is there a legal instrument evidencing such ownership? The land law setting a period for the registration of customary land, that period, was it observed in this case? Finally, what was the legal status of the Cdc and the land it operates on at the time of Reunification ?"

And Maurice Kamto continuing (2003: 313):

> "If it turns out that the famous 1947 arrangement has existed and has never been repealed or stated, then one should admit the validity of claims made. Otherwise, we will argue that the lands in question are part of the national domain and can be classified in whole or in part within the private domain of the State, the said domain property being alienated."

The reaction of the Bakweri at the announcement of the privatization of the Cdc sparked another reaction, that of the Cameroon State.

REACTION BEFORE A REACTION

The position of the cameroonian government, could not be more ambiguous. Indeed, since the land claims of the Bakweri, the cameroonian government does not officially take a position, if not maintain blur, better silent about the land issue. This position, can it be understood as a government strategy?

Following the Memorandum[2] of the Bakweri community of August 4th, 1994, President Paul Biya had decided to send a delegation led by Mr. Ephraim Inoni[3], a native Bakweri, then Secretary General at the Presidency, to discuss the land issue. It was acknowledged that the government should have come into contact with the Bakweri before the announcement of the privatization of the Cdc[4]. "Mea culpa" or simple tactic? Hard to say. Still, since then, the government has never discussed the problem with the Bakweri. "*After the government delegation returned to Yaounde, writes Piet Konings[5], "no further government action took place concerning Cdc privatization but this apparent victory for Anglophone resistance turned out to be short-lived [. . .] The Cdc was finally put up for sale in 1999.*"

Decided to go through, Blcc sent an open letter[6] to potential buyers of the CDC, in these terms: "*It is our duty to advise you to think twice before you commit the resources of your shareholders in a venture that is still mired in controversy and whose promised financial and economic rewards may prove to be illusory in the long run.*"

2. Memorandum of the Bakweri People on the Presidential Decree to privatize or Sell Cameroon Development Corporation, Buea, 27th July 1994.

3. Piet Konings, "Privatization and ethno-regional protest," 16.

4. Piet Konings, "Privatization and ethno-regional protest," 16.

5. Piet Konings, "Privatization and ethno-regional protest," 17.

6. Blcc, "Open Letter to All Prospective Buyers of Cdc Plantations", Buea, 12 October 2000 Cited by Piet Konings, "Privatization and ethno-regional protest in Cameroon," 18.

Failing to respond formally to the reaction of Bakweri, an attitude adopted by the government, was to appoint a Bakweri, above all General Manager of Cdc, as Prime Minister, in the person of Peter Mafany Musonge. Was it an opportunity for the government to accelerate the privatization of the Cdc? Surely, since the Blcc saw it increasingly difficult to take action on the national level, with a Prime minister native of Fako. According to Piet Konings[7] :

> "It became increasingly evident that the Blcc was finding it hard to defend Bakweri Interests at the national level after 'their own son', Peter Mafany Musonge, then the general manager of the Cdc, was appointed prime minister in 1996. Without doubt, one of the reasons for his appointment to this position was that President Biya Regarded him, being an ex-Cdc general manager and a Bakweri, as the most suitable candidate to handle the delicate issue of Cdc privatization."

Subsequently we know, Musonge could not resolve the difficult question of the privatization of the Cdc. His successor, another Bakweri will he be up to the task? We think is not the problem because the solution should reside in the status of exploited land by the Cdc. We agree with Maurice Kamto (2003: 313), for whom:

> "The intervention by public authorities on this issue still leave some perplexity, rumour and the lack of an official position on this issue publicly affirmed by the bed of speculation. Although it is said that the decision to privatize the Cdc is irreversible, takeover counting bids have been maintained on January 2nd, 2001, one wonders what is meant when the head of privatization at the representation of the World bank said in Yaounde—to explain the slow operation—that people have taken time to understand that Cdc privatization is not a sale of the land. Would it then just be selling of trees and crops?"

Given the slow pace of privatization of the Cdc announced in 1994, it would be difficult to find a solution to the problem, as the cameroonian authorities, representatives of the employees of the

---

7. Piet Konings, Privatization and ethno-regional protest, "18–9.

Cdc and the representatives of the Bakweri community will not agree on a social compromise.

TOWARDS A SOCIAL COMPROMISE?

"Any conjuncture difficulty, writes Jean Paul Ngoupande (1994: 9), does not mean a situation of crisis [...] Simple difficulties along the way to deal with remedies for the occasion, while situations of crisis require the rethinking of the very foundations of social structure, and that from there we rebuild".

The search for a social compromise could lead to a favourable outcome of the problem, if the needs of employees and those of the Bakweri people are taken into consideration by the cameroonian authorities.

Every public policy should indeed be that of the logic of a "*social construct*" that takes into account the values, the behaviours of social actors. Understanding public policies go through all that is important—in the case of the Cdc—to consider the social and political impact of the texts on populations to which this policy applies. Here lies the real stake of public policies on the privatization of State and para-public enterprises.

This compromise requires understanding of the terms of agro-land reform, agrarian reform and land reform depending on whether we are in the anglo-saxon conception or in the Latin design.

The agro-land reform "*changes the nature of titles held on space*" (E. Le Bris et alii., 1982: 29) agrarian *reform "redistributes space between producers*" (E. Le Bris et alii., 1982: 29) while "*land reform poses the problem of the surface on which this law applies*"(E. Le Bris et alii., 1982: 29). If land reform may appear alone, we cannot talk about agrarian reform without this being accompanied by a redistribution of land titles (E. Le Bris et alii., 1982: 29). Everything ultimately depends on the objective. In Togo, for example, the government opted for an agro-land reform aimed at agricultural productivity, while in neighbouring Benin, there was a policy aiming at agrarian reform, the release of land. In other words, the problem is primarily a problem of political choice. In the present context is that of the Cdc, there is no evidence that the cameroonian government had changed the status of land operated by this company. These lands are still part of the private sector (as reported in "Grundbuch" land) until proven otherwise. Solving this problem will not be easy as it will seek to make some concessions. In addition, even if the Bakweri collective through their Blcc Committee, wants to address the land issue with the cameroonian government peacefully, all indications are that on the government's side, the time is not yet trading. For proof, several failed attempts made by the Blcc to address the issue with government authorities. At this stage of the problem, it is hard not to seek for a social compromise, given the seriousness of the situation, especially because of the position of the "African Commission on Human Rights" asking authorities in Yaounde, to temporarily suspend the privatization of the Cdc.

In addition to the Bakweri land claims, privatization poses the problem of land tenure in Africa.

The Question of Land Tenure in Africa: What Place to Give to the Practices of Actors?

> "Land is a day to day battle, a battle without rest: clearing, planting, weeding, watering, till harvesting, and then you see your mature field lying in front of you in the morning, with dew and you say: me, such, governor of the dew . . . " Jacques Roumain, Governeur de la rosée. Quoted by Albert Tevoédjré, La pauvreté, richesse des peuples, (1978: 72.)

The land issue in Black Africa is a real problem since ages. It has several angles of approach, possible assumptions and stakes.

One particular approach angle is one that *"gives privilege to the perspective of concrete actors and groups of actors to report land practices"* (Jean-Pierre Chauveau 1998: 36). This approach is that of strategic analysis, interactionist, which considers the relationship between men and groups about access to land and its use. This is the approach that we have convened partly in the study. An alternative approach is one that focuses on the relationship between different modes of access and use of land (legal approach angle). The other angle is that of normative approach on the relationship between different modes of access and use established and those that should prevail to achieve a goal: the level of agro-economic performance, fairness, and social peace (Jean-Pierre Chauveau 1998: 36).

As possible hypotheses for the analysis of the land question in Black Africa, we can note:

Land phenomenon as a phenomenon of social and historical order;

Relations between men and land.

But beyond hypotheses, it is necessary to raise some stakes. Thereof are numerous, and often political and economic, nay even social. *"The stakes of a land policy, write Jean-Pierre Chauveau and Paul Mathieu (1998: 261), cannot be reduced to issues of agricultural development. Control of land and resources is (and most of all) a stake to power. Historically, colonial laws on land and national resources have been instruments of dispossession of local communities . . . "*

It is clear from this analysis that African States inherited an anglophone , francophone, lusophone colonial legislation depending on the country. Hence, the legal pluralism that appears there, when States could not impose a standard.

Zimbabwe's agrarian reforms led to release of land taken away by white farmers, from their former owners, the indigenous. The backlash that followed the dispossession show how the land issue is highly sensitive. The israeli-palestinian problem is an example. In other countries such as South Africa, Kenya, Namibia, political authorities are very cautious about the way of posing the problem. Thus, the land issue is closely linked to that of the State and the question of relations between States, the political and administrative elites, local elites and populations. Several observations can be made on:

83

Legalism that affects the vocabulary or a certain approach to reality, it is for example the words 'land' and 'property';

Place assumed by the State in the development of a new discourse
on the issue, as well as the orientation of social practices and
behavioural evolution;

The ratio of national economies in the global market.

> "The current land problems, write E. Le Bris et al., (1982:
> 26) fits into two processes, one for the extension of State
> intervention and the other for the spread of capitalism,
> these two processes are linked in a complex dynamic [
> . . .] the State appears as the central player in land strate-
> gies, one that, by her 'weight' necessarily affects the oth-
> ers. The gradual spread of capitalism in the countryside
> and its introduction to new places of production is also
> the highlight of the last 20 years. Urban and coastal
> phenomenon during the colonial period, capitalism
> becomes widespread and affects behaviour in a globalist
> logic".

Considering these remarks is an opportunity for African
countries in general and Cameroon in particular, to pave the way
for new social bases grounded on a State of law. This implies State
intervention. Regarding Cameroon, we wonder if government intervention is inevitable.

STATE INTERVENTION, IS IT INEVITABLE?

For Abdelilah Hamdouch (1989: 256), depending on whether
the State decides to privatize or nationalize a company remains a
"*State of influence*", although often, decisions come from external
pressures.

"Beyond the political power, writes Abdelilah Hamdouch
(1989: 10), and various orientations of State interventionism over
time, the relationship between big companies and the State seem
indeed characterized by a constant: the permanence of that which
might be called the State of influence. "The State of influence puts
us in a kind of political labyrinth where the blur is enabled. For

Abdelilah Hamdouch, "the concept of State of influence refers to the set of relations more or less shady, often moving and complex that big companies and the various bodies of the State have." (1989: 12). Indeed, when we seek to understand the logic behind privatization policies, it is clear that clarity is not always an accepted principle. The State of emergence is a mixture of genres.

> "It is born from the combination of two processes. The first is the one that brought the State to become a prominent player in the economy both as a shareholder and as an entrepreneur and as the main contractor for the development of the entire production system."

As for the second, "*it covers the mutations of structures of french capitalism.* "These structures may be analyzed to varying degrees. In terms of its characteristics and financial organizations, mechanisms of captation and its mutations.

At the first level it must be said that the characteristics and financial organizations of french capitalism determine the location of economic power. At the second level, it is clear the presence of mechanisms for captation and exercise of that power. Here, the presence of men forming the junction between the State of influence and capitalism of influence is very strong. Capitalism of influence! It is in these terms that could be called french capitalism. Cameroon, as many African States, being part of the french pre-square. This capitalism of influence is reflected in facts of several manners. It favours for example the relational to structural. Abdelilah Hamdouch (1989: 232) notes to this effect that:

> "After being the State of nascent and triumphant capitalism, then of 'poised' capitalism of social compromise, it seems to have turned into a 'manager' of the mutant change, whose structures are both more complex and bastardized [. . .] Emphasizing the relationship to the detriment of the structural, french capitalism has gradually evolved into capitalism of influence where economic power is from sources other than those exclusively related to fortune."

85

We are not saying that it is France that calls on Cameroon to privatize. These are international institutions with the support of other countries including France, the European Union, etc. At the last level, you have to simply identify recent changes and allocation procedures of economic power. It is by purpose that we had spoken of political maze, because economics is not always master of its choice. In other words, the transparency of privatization may seem vain. For proof, in the years 1986-1987, the French were surprised to see *"the interference of political game in the privatization process,"* in the words of Zaki Laïdi. The State of influence can indeed go hand in hand with capitalism of influence. Better, it is reinforced by the said capitalism. It is a State, nay even *"a kingdom where influence is king."* This influence is more evident with State liberalism that appeals not only to relations between the State and the corporate world, but also with the world, said of business.

We think, with Jean-Marie Atangana Mebara, that one of the stakes of privatization policies is the idea according to which the more a country is colonized better it will seek to appeal (A. Hamdouch 1989: 232) to companies of the colonizing power. Cameroon is a country of the french square (we repeat)! In other words, french companies have more room reserved for them than companies of other powers. The very choice of companies is in itself a major stake. However, we express the faintest difference in our remarks by noting that there aren't only companies of the colonizing power to which States appeal. Increasingly, we find foreign companies who have no connection with the colonizing power. This is for example the case of Aes Sonel with the Americans, for the privatization of the electricity sector in Cameroon.

The announced privatization of the Cdc puts us in a different kind of privatization, namely industrial privatization. This *"raises, according to Vincent Wright (1993: 21), different questions, involves different actors and different policy networks, is motivated by different goals and generates different constraints."*

How to conciliate the different positions? Important issue that should allow different stakeholders to find a social compromise that would be considered as a new social contract for life in society. The resolution of the land problem in Fako division goes through this.

GENERAL CONCLUSION

At the end of our study, it seems on the one hand clear that a close link exists between the position of people from Fako division and the Northwest , and on the other hand the delay in the privatization of the Cdc, announced more than 20 years ago. Indeed, the idea of privatizing a public company in Cameroon had never met much opposition as that of privatising the Cdc.

With 13,000 employees, the second largest employer after the Cameroon State is indeed the reason for living of the people of the Southwest and Northwest. Since its inception in 1947, the Cdc has supported generations of families who increasingly fear its dismantling. In this sense, it is a "social" company that does not only exploit the natural resources of the country, but makes live her people. She provides employees with essential social services through schools, clinics and housing. Difficult to ask a private company to continue performing such services. In addition, native Bakweri do not appreciate the exploitation of their land by a private company. Grouped into the collective "Bakweri Land Claims Committee" (Blcc), they request the return of their ancestral lands.

Placed on the side of public policy, we analyzed how most of the time, these policies do not sufficiently take into account the needs and interests of the people. Our study is based on responses raised by these populations over certain decisions of public policy. We chose a company in the agro-industrial sector. This study is structured around the following question: *"How to conciliate profit with the social dimension of privatization? Specifically, with regard to the privatization of the Cdc, for example, how can the Cameroon government continue the process of privatization, without alienating the social achievements of workers and lands of the indigenous, the Bakweri?"*

A sample of 114 people enabled us to address the issue. Given the multiplicity of actors, we decided to approach the subject from the side of those who make claims, the Bakweri being at the fore front; the side of those who provide great labour force, that is to say the Northwest nationals; and finally the side of Cdc workers. Other actors being the cameroonian government, the Bretton Woods institutions, and the African Commission on Human Rights (on which we recognize not having much insisted).

If *"the stake with regard to government interventions in territories is very justified and supported by specialists of development, especially those in urban and regional economics, economic geography and local public economics" (Marc-Urbain Proul 2002: 104)*, it appears as shown by our analysis that the Cameroon government should focus more on concerted public decisions, negotiated, and not those taken unilaterally.

Our analysis also allowed us to realize that a close link exists between the political, the economic and the social dimension of privatization. The strategic and interactionist analyses we convened, confirmed our primary hypothesis. Namely: *economic liberalization accompanying the privatization of the Cdc may, undoubtedly, be an operation of promotion of economic democracy, if it involves employers, workers, public authorities and indigenous populations in the search of appropriate strategies and methods.* We noticed that failure to involve all stakeholders created a major problem in the smooth running of the process of privatization of the Cdc. The demands of the people of the Southwest and Northwest explain the delay witnessed by this company.

This privatization is a very sensitive issue because of its relation to the land problem never resolved first by the german colonists, then by the cameroonian authorities. And the fact that the Cdc nourished over 13,000 families of the regions mentioned, shows both the political and the social sensitivity of the problem.

Regarding the social dimension, we found that the Cdc has several health, educational facilities, and that privatization would jeopardize the continuation of this social function. We chose as an example the Cameroon Tea Estates (CTE) to show that this social function ceased being considered, once the tea industry was privatized.

Since the issue of privatization of the Cdc raises the question of the nature of the lands this company operates on, we have shown that at this level, a real problem exists. The lands used by the Cdc were taken away by german settlers from native Bakweri without compensation. The State ignored this aspect of the problem, deciding to privatize the largest agro-business company, without having foreseen the consequences that such a decision could cause. It is no coincidence that the government decided to create a Ministry of Land and State affairs. Thus, these observations confirm our secondary hypothesis: *the privatization of the Cdc is now presented as a major option that goes beyond the framework of the economy.* As proof, the cameroonian political authorities seem to have appointed two successive Bakweri sons (Peter Mafany Musonge, former General Manager of the Cdc and Ephraim Inoni) as Prime minister, to facilitate its privatization. Things getting complicated as the native Bakweri adopted a strategy of making the international community and potential buyers of the Cdc aware, given the seriousness of the problem. In addition, they sought a meeting with the government to find a positive and peaceful solution to the land issue. Announced more than 20 years ago, the Cdc privatization remains to be done. Meanwhile, the land claims of native Bakweri blocked and still block the privatization of this mega structure.

In addition, the analysis of the data of our survey confirms another secondary hypothesis raised at the beginning of our study, namely: *the privatization of Cdc will induce significant social impact on employment, workers' status, labour law and the ancestral lands of indigenous peoples.* On the one hand, the Blcc called on the African Commission on Human Rights, to question the State of Cameroon (signatory of laws governing it). After reviewing the record, the Commission asked the public authorities in Yaounde, to suspend the privatization of the Cdc, pending a favourable outcome of the land issue. On the other hand, Northwest nationals (the greatest labour force of the Cdc) joined the Bakweri to lead the same fight. To the best of our knowledge, the government did not take an official position.

Having analysed the social implications of the privatization of the Cdc, we think it's essential to make some suggestions that may be useful to different social actors, for a social compromise:

1. a joint committee of members of government and those of the Bakweri collective, should be formed to study thoroughly the land issue;

2. another joint committee of members of government, Bakweri natives and Northwest nationals, looking at the possible social consequences that the privatization of the Cdc could result into;

3. a review of documents on land and state regime, in regard to the lands used by the Cdc, be done. The government must make it clear if these lands are still part of the private domain, or are no more. The creation of a Ministry of Land and State Affairs may allow us to demonstrate the impact of land issues, beyond the case of the Cdc;

4. that the government, more and more, involves people in decisions on public policy in order to avoid duplication of reactions such as those inherent in the privatization of the Cdc. Such reactions create a social malaise that does not promote coexistence between the different actors involved in a policy of privatization.

The analysis of public policy in Africa in general and Cameroon in particular, would benefit from reconciling more and more the political, economic and social dimension in the field of privatization policies. Not only does it create a favourable climate among different actors, but also, it would facilitate the privatization of several companies.

Blcc would normally find a favourable solution before the government. Not having found a listening ear before german settlers, will it witness the same scenario? Indeed, everything happens as if at the level of those who decide, the actor just changed the skin; the victim staying the same. Who decides finally? Is it the State or the Bretton Woods institutions? Both could tell us, to the extent where States are free and sovereign. At the same time, the World Bank and IMF will mount pressure on States in such a way as to impose their logic.

Appendix 1

Questions for people living in Limbe

Date:

Place:

No:

Name:

Sex:

Married:

Job:

School level:

> Primary school
> Secondary school
> University

Age:

> 18-30 years old
> 31-40 years old
> 41-50 years old
> More than 50 years old

1. What do you know about CDC (Cameroon Development Corporation)?

2. Have you heard about the BLCC (Bakweri Land Claims Committee)?

3. To you, who are the landowners on which CDC operates?

4. What does privatization mean for you?

5. Do you think that the idea of privatizing public enterprises is a good idea?

6. Why?

7. What do you think about the privatization of public enterprises in Cameroon?

8. What do you think about the privatization of CDC?

9. Do you know Bakweri people? Who are they?

Appendix 2

Questions for CDC workers

Date:

Place:

No:

Name:

Sex:

Married:

Job:

School level:

       Primary school
       Secondary school
       University

Age:

       18-30 years old
       31-40 years old
       41-50 years old
       More than 50 years old

1. For how long have you been working with CDC?
2. What are the daily problems in your job?

3. How do you identify them?

4. Did these problems change with the time?

5. How?

6. Are you optimistic for the future?

7. What does privatization mean for you?

8. Do you think that the idea of privatizing public enterprises is a good idea?

9. Why?

Appendix 3

Questions for CDC workers

Date:

Place:

No:

Name:

Sex:

Married:

Job:

School level:

       Primary school
       Secondary school
       University

Age:

       18-30 years old
       31-40 years old
       41-50 years old
       More than 50 years old

1. What do you think about the privatization of public enterprises in Cameroon?
2. What do you think about the privatization of CDC?

3. Do you know Bakweri people?

4. Who are they?

5. What do you expect from CDC?

6. What do you expect from the government about the idea of privatizing CDC?

7. Have you heard about the "BLCC" (Bakweri Land Claims Committee)?

8. Who are the landowners on which "CDC" operates?

9. What is your relationship with the population?

10. What is your relationship with "Bakweri" people?

11. What is the role of CDC in the South-West Province?

12. What does CDC represent for you?

Appendix 4

Questions for Bakweri people

Date:

Place:

No:

Name:

Sex:

Married:

Job:

School level:

Primary school
Secondary school
University

Age:

18-30 years old
31-40 years old
41-50 years old
More than 50 years old

1. Who are the landowners on which CDC operates?
2. Are you sure that the land on which CDC operates is yours?

3. How?

4. What is the meaning of the land in your culture (tradition)?

5. Do you have a traditional chief?

6. How do you call the "land" in your language?

7. How do you call the government in your language?

8. How is your relationship with the government?

Appendix 5

Memorandum of the Bakweri

MEMORANDUM OF THE BAKWERI PEOPLE ON THE PRESIDENTIAL DECREE TO PRIVATISE OR SELL THE CAMEROON DEVELOPMENT CORPORATION.

PREAMBLE

ONE'S HISTORY IS PART of his present. The Cameroon Development Corporation ("CDC") is the history of Cameroon and of the Bakweri people, in particular. For them, if for no one else, this public institution remains an integral and vital part of their present, a poignant reminder of their long and arduous struggle to reclaim lands which were forcibly expropriated from them during a period of ruthless German imperial occupation (circa 1896-1914); of petitions, remonstrations and representations here and abroad.[1] This then is the context within which one can begin to understand and appreciate the shock waves that swept through every nook and

1. [See e.g.: Petition of the Bakweri Land Claims Committee to the Trusteeship council, U.N.O. Doc. T/PET.4.3, Report of the Trusteeship Visiting Mission, 1949; English Commission of Inquiry, Notice N° 90 West Gazette N° 13, 1st April 1967; the Endeley-Burnley-Mukete Memprandum on Land Tenure and Problems Resulting From Ruthless Alienation of Lands in Fako Division, Sept. 17, 1973]

cranny of Bakweri society following the recent announcement in the French language news of Government's intention to privatise or sell the CDC.

There comes a time when even the most compliant people must rise up in righteous indignation and declare "ENOUGH IS ENOUGH." Our silence in the face of persistent and systematic abuse and misuse of our patrimony by others has been mistaken for weakness, our generosity misconstrued as stupidity and our civility dismissed as docility. We, the signatories of this document, the accredited representatives of thousands of Bakweri, on whose rich and fertile soils the CDC has been operating for close to half a century, have been authorised to proclaim loudly and clearly that the dismantling of this core institution will have an adverse and disproportionate impact on the indigenes (sic) of Fako Division. Because we believe that this decision is wrong, it must be reversed, now. We reach this painful conclusion after sober reflection and exhaustive discussion among our people and only after they have convinced us that further silence over the continued assault on our individual and collective existence is no longer in our best interests, present and future. On their behalf, therefore, we shall attempt to present the Bakweri case for legal title over ancestral lands which since 1946 (sic) were taken over by the CDC on a tenancy for a period and to explain why the Bakweri now stand firm, resolute and united in their opposition to any attempt to dispossess them once again of these lands through legal manoeuvres.

PRIVATISATION IN CONTEXT

In principle, the Bakweri have no quarrel with the idea of privatisation or sale of companies in which government enjoys majority control since we fully understand the logic behind such an exercise, i.e., the relocation of the management of inefficiently managed parastatals in more efficient hands. We recognise that Government, as the controlling shareholder in these companies, has an obligation to the majority shareholders and the Cameroonian taxpayer to ensure that their tax revenues are not wasted on failing parastatals. Should Government, in the discharge of its fiduciary obligations to these various constituencies, eject to dispose of its majority interests for fair consideration to private purchasers, in order to spare the ordinary Cameroonian the burden of subsidising these white elephants, we offer our full support. While we believe that the medicine proposed to cure companies like SOTUC, Cameroon Airlines, SOCAPALM may be appropriate for their particular ailment, it is, however, most inappropriate for the CDC. Our strong opposition to the privatisation or sale of the CDC is two-fold. First, we remain unconvinced that as a disciplinary mechanism for correcting inefficiently managed companies, privatisation should be applied to a corporation, which by ail objective indicators is efficiently managed. Moreover, even though the corporation has in the recent past gone through a period of severe economic strain, available evidence paint a portrait of an organisation on the rebound.

Privatisation or sale, as ordinarily understood, involves the transfer to new owners of all or substantially all of the property and assets of the target company; airplanes, buildings, goodwill and so on. In the case of the CDC, a sale will result in its plantations and lands being taken over by private interests. The problem here is that the CDC does not own the lands on which its plantations occupy and cannot, therefore, transfer what it does not have. Herein lies our second objection to Government's announced privatisation policy as pertains to the CDC. The lands occupied by the corporation were forcibly expropriated by the Germans from their original owners, the Bakweri. With the end of German imperial rule, theses former German Plantation Estates passed to the successor British colonial administration who held them as native [read: Bakweri] lands. The lands were subsequently leased to the newly-incorporated CDC in 1946 for a period of 60 years on terms which expressly provided for reversionary rights in the Administering Authority upon the expiration of the corporations lease. That title to these lands never passed to the CDC and that the Administering Authority as well as the successor independent Cameroon Government was acting only as custodian, holding them in trust for present and future generations of Bakweri people, is so well known and memorialised in countless legal instruments and official documents[2] that a detailed review is unnecessary. Suffice to say that the Bakweri did not, could not and would not have transferred **395 square miles** (104, 000 hectares) of their most fertile parcels of land—representing roughly two-thirds of their total land area[3]—to the CDC for nothing! Indeed, the CDC itself recognised that it had only temporary use and occupation of these lands and made provisions in its books for annual payment of ground rents. Furthermore, the corporation willingly participated in exercises that resulted in the excising from the plantation areas it leased lands for use by land-squeezed indigenous inhabitants without as much asking for compensation.

It should be recalled that when the Bakweri dropped their long-standing land claims and gave their consent to the creation of the CDC, it was with the express understanding that while the lands would be developed for the common benefit of ail English-speaking Cameroonians, the ground rents the corporation agreed to pay to Government would be used for the exclusive benefit of the Bakweri landowners. In its almost 50 years of operation the CDC has lived up to this mandate, developing the rich natural resources of Fako Division on a scale unprecedented in our nation's history. As we have already indicated, it is a matter of public record that the corporation set aside annually an amount it paid into the public treasury as ground rents though precious little ever reached the Bakweri!

Given its unique place in modem Cameroon history, the CDC cannot be, and has never been, equated with an ordinary business enterprise the likes of SOTUC, SOCAPALM, CAMAIR, etc. The CDC is no run-of-the-mill commercial operation but a public institution upon which was conferred an historical obligation to assume a leadership role, in partnership with Government,

2. See e.g., Article 8 of the Trusteeship Agreement; sec. 4 of the ex-Enemy Lands (Cameroon) Ordinance, N° 38 of 1946; Ex-Enemy Lands (Likomba Estates) Ordinance, N°22 of 1947; and sec., 3 of the Land and Native Rights Ordinance, cap. 96 of the 1958 edition of the Laws of Nigeria.

3. See Annual Report of Cameroons Under United Kingdom Administration, 1956, p. 60 at para. 302.

in the socio-economic development of our nation. In order not to compromise this mission, the statute setting up the CDC deliberately excluded private shareholders from equity—participation for fear that their single-minded pursuit of profits may push the corporation farther away from the broad social objectives it was by statute expected to fulfil. Thus, the attempt to twin SOTUC or CAMAIR and the CDC is misplaced and confuses their respective roles in our society. Indeed, to treat both as same is to invite ridicule or anger, as the case may be, from those who know what CDC has been to Cameroon's economic development. Clarity and good logic dictate that an ordinary profit-making enterprise like Cameroon Airlines must not be confused with a public institution like CDC whose presence is felt in 1 aspects of national life. It follows therefore that the criteria employed for rationalising the privatisation or sale of the assets of the typical commercial company do not apply pari passu to the CDC.

DIRECT EFFECTS OF THE DISMANTLING OF CDC ON THE BAKWERI

The point bears repeating that in creating the CDC the colonial administration sought to strike a careful balance between two competing interests: on one hand, to protect the interests of the Bakweri in their lands while, on the other, ensuring that these lands can be properly and efficiently managed for the common good of all.[4] It is clear to us that the proposed scheme to privatise the CDC conflicts with the original and enduring policy rationale for its establishment in the first place. Implementing this proposal would amount to a betrayal by Government of the undertakings it made to the community of nations at the time of independence. Moreover, allowing the CDC to be taken over by third parties would signal the abdication of the fiduciary duty Government owes to the Bakweri people in particular and ail Cameroonians in general.

4. See Cameroons Development Corporation Ordinance, number 39 of 1946.

We note in passing that in the typical sale of assets of a business enterprise, its officers and directors have a fiduciary duty to take into account the best interests of the company, meaning its shareholders. And here, the calculation of 'best interests' is a simple arithmetic exercise as to whether the price offered for the company stock exceeds its present market value. However, in the case of public institution such as the CDC, the calculation of best interests gores beyond merely getting the best price for the corporation's stock. Government as the fiduciary, by virtue of its majority interests, has a clear duty to consider the effects of a sale—short-term and long range, material as well as psychological—on CDC employees, their families and the communities in which the corporation maintains a presence.

Above all, the interests of the Bakweri people without whose lands there would have been no CDC in the first place must forever remain paramount. These interests will surely be sacrificed by a sale which effectively transfers two-thirds of Bakweri land area to private non-native owners whose interests might not be in concert with ours. We have no illusions as to the likely consequences of the transfer of CDC to private ownership. If it goes through, it threatens to alter irrevocably existing land holding arrangements and the pattern of natural resource exploitation in Fako Division. We face the very likely break-up of the large CDC plantations into small private plots under non-native control which may be operated under a different economic development logic. Deprived of, and denied access to, the ancestral lands, generations of Bakweri will never know or appreciate the meaning of land ownership. Given the cramped conditions under Which Bakweri currently live—where the CDC appropriated itself some 400 square miles the Bakweri, all 50,000 of them, are confined to less than 150 square miles of the land space—a forced exodus of our members to other parts of Cameroon in search of more salubrious land for farming and housing is likely to follow in the wake of the sale or privatisation of the CDC. The likelihood that other compatriots may not be as charitable to these migrants Bakweri as we have been to immigrants who have settled in our communities is very real indeed.

This, the risk of exporting the social tensions that have historically characterised settler-native relations in Fako Division cannot be ignored. Can the government in good conscience close its eyes to this imminent threat to public order and social tranquillity?

INTERNATIONAL IMPLICATIONS

It is tempting to treat Government's announced intention to privatise or sell the CDC as a purely local affair but we believe that it has far-reaching implications that go well beyond our national borders. Progressive development and codification of international law has now reached the stage where collective or individual land ownership by indigenous minorities is recognised and protected as a fundamental human rights violation of which imposes on states a duty of reparation. Cameroon is a member of the United nations [admitted **on Sept. 20, under charter Article 4**], a member of the Organisation of African Unity [interred **into force Sept. 13, 1963**], an aspiring member of the Commonwealth of Nations, and a signatory or party to all pertinent human rights instruments that address this question of minority land ownership rights. For instance the **1966 International Covenant on Economic Social and Cultural Rights**, to which Cameroon became a signatory on June 27, 1984 and which had earlier come into force on January 3, 1976, enjoins by its article 25 States parties from impairing the inherent right of all peoples to enjoy and utilise fully and freely their natural wealth and resources.

In the same vein, Article 11 of the **1957 International Labour Organisation Convention ("ILO") (No. 107) Concerning the Protection and Integration of Indigenous and other Tribal and Semi-Tribal Populations in Independent Countries, and Article 14 of the 1989 ILO Convention (No. 169) on Indigenous and Tribal Peoples in Independent Countries, revising the 1957 ILO Convention (No. 107)**, both recognise and protect the right of collective and individual ownership, possession and use, of an indigenous people, such as the Bakweri, of the lands or resources which their members have traditionally occupied or used and further provide for their right to compensation for lands expropriated by Government. [15 ILO Convention (169)]. These international human rights instruments expressly bind government to "respect the special importance for the cultures and spiritual values" of indigenous peoples "of their relationship with the lands and territories . . . which they occupy or otherwise use, and in particular the collective aspects of this relationship." [13 ILO Convention (No. 169)] Although Cameroon was never a party to the 1957 ILO Convention (No.107) and has not yet acceded to the 1989 ILO convention (169), their provisions have through the passage of time and the consistent practice of States entered through the body of customary international law and are binding even on those nations that have net signed them.

While we are not in the habit of issuing threats, we wish to serve notice of our resolve to pursue this matter in all for a open to us including, if necessary, the United Nations until we are vindicated. Towards this end, it is our intention to brief and instruct counsel to lodge an appeal on our behalf before the **U.N. Sub-Commission on Prevention of Discrimination and Protection of Minorities through its Working Group on Indigenous Populations (established by the United Nation Economic and Social Council—ECOSOC—in** 1982 to promote and protect the human rights of indigenous people).

LEARNING FROM THE EXPERIENCE OF OTHER NATIONS

The Bakweri are not alone in this struggle to regain control over their ancestral lands. They are joined by numerous indigenous minority groups in other parts of the globe [**Kikuyus in Kenya, the native Indians of North America, the Chiapas of Mexico, the Miskito of Nicaragua, the Mabo of Australia,** to mention but a few] who sought restitution of indigenous land whether taken by conquest, in violation of treaty obligations or through "legal" alienation and from whose valiant struggles they draw inspiration. While many of these earlier struggles resulted in the spilling of priceless blood and the loss of lives, we intend to conduct our campaign in a peaceful, non-violent and dignified manner taking our cue from the protracted negotiations between the Canadian Government and its minority native populations. In this regard, we wish to draw Government's attention to recent Canadian legislation pursuant to the James Bay and Northern Quebec agreement among the Cree's, Inuit, the provincial government of Quebec, and the federal government. The **Cree-Naspaki Act of 1984** leaves basic ownership of Indian lands in the hands of Quebec, but the **exclusive use and benefit of the land and its natural resources** remains with the Indians. The agreement provides for an Indian entity to administer, manage and use these lands and resources as though it were the owner. Although the provincial government of Quebec owns all mineral and subsurface rights, it must secure Indian permission to exploit these resources and it must compensate the Indians for their use. Confronted with the vexing and sensitive issue of lands expropriated from its indigenous minority populations which threatened to shred to pieces the delicate tapestry of national unity, the Canadian government did not flinch but responded with an enlightened and humane policy carefully crafted to strike a happy balance among competing subnational interests. Because of our firm belief that our Government can do better, we now urge it to rethink its announced policy to privatise or sell the CDC drawing heavily from the recent experiences of Canada and Mexico (with respect to the Chiapa Indians).

FRAMEWORK FOR CONSTRUCTIVE DIALOGUE BETWEEN GOVERNMENT AND THE BAKWERI

We would remiss in our duty and open to charges of unpatriotism if we ended this memorandum without advancing some concrete proposals to assist Government in formulating a wise and sound decision on the question of privatising the CDC. It is our belief that no government committed to the principles of justice, fairness and equality can, at this stage in the development of international human rights law, proceed by fiat to disposes a distinct segment of its population of two-thirds of its total land area without even the courtesy of discussing the matter with the leaders of that ethnic group. As a consequence, we insist that as a first step Government should meet with the accredited representatives of the Bakweri people—and we stress accredited spokesmen p externally-imposed interlocutors out for their own selfish mercenary interests—to work out the modalities of transferring the assets and property of the CDC, if it must come to this, to the rightful owners of the land.

Second, there must be explicit acknowledgment by Government that the lands occupied by the CDC having been declared native lands by virtue of the **Land and Native Rights Ordinance, the Ex-Enemy Lands (Cameroon) Ordinance, and the Ex-Enemy Lands (Likomba Estates) Ordinance,** reverted to the indigenous natives of Fako Division in 1946 and ownership legally vested in them.

Third, because the CDC is so vital to our economic life, it must be maintained at all costs. In this vein, we propose a creative and enlightened partnership between the owners of the land on which the corporation operates and the providers of finance capital without which it would not be possible to run a modem, technologically sophisticated agro-commercial complex like the CDC. If for economic reasons private cash capital has to be attracted (one of the ostensible reasons for privatisation), it should be on terms which recognise the ownership of land as a distinct variable which together with the cash make plantation agriculture possible. Therefore, landowners deserve ground rent compensation in much the same way as the CDC was liable to pay ground rents for the use of the land. Furthermore, if the excuse for establishing a statutory public corporation in 1946 was the lack of available indigenous personnel competent to obtain maximum benefit from the erstwhile German estates, that excuse is no longer tenable. There is now a surfeit of trained Fako indigenes from which to recruit competent technical and managerial experts who can profitably run the CDC.

Finally, since a renascent CDC will be jointly-owned and managed by the landowners and capital providers, it follows logically that the former must be represented on the policy-making organs of the corporation in numbers sufficient to reflect their equal contribution. History teaches us that only a significant presence of landowners in policy-making organs can prevent the ruthless discrimination against indigenous in matters of employment and promotion that has been the corporation's past practice.

DONE AT BUEA THIS 27TH DAY OF JULY
IN THE YEAR OF OUR LORD NINETEEN
HUNDRED AND NINETY-FOUR
ON BEHALF OF THE BAKWERI PEOPLE
H.R.H. SAM M. L. ENDELEY

Paramount Chief of Buea

H.R.H. BILLE F. MANGA WILLIAMS

Paramount Chief of Victoria

ON BEHALF OF THE BAKWERI LAND
COMMITTE
CHIEF PHILIP MOFEMA EWUSI
ON BEHALF OF THE AD HOC COMMITTEE

DR. S.N. LYONGA, Chairman
PROF. NDIVA KOFELEKALE, Secretary

Appendix 6

Letter of BLCC-USA to BLCC-Fako

BAKWERI LAND CLAIMS COMMITTEE–USA (BLCC-USA)
P.O. BOX 433
ORONO, MAINE, 04473 USA
To Their Royal Highnesses. The Chiefs of Fako Division, Southwest
Province. Cameroon.

March 15, 2001

Your Royal Highnesses,

We, your children, the Fako elements living in all continents of the world, and involved in all kinds of professions, meeting together through the wonderful global technology of the Internet, have the honor to present our high regards to your excellencies. We write you today on a matter of extreme urgency and importance for the Bakweri people as a whole and the future generation of our community. The matter at hand is the imminent privatization of the Cameroon Development Corporation (CDC) without due consultation of the Bakweri who are the rightful owners of the lands currently being exploited by the CDC.

Before explaining our stance on this urgent matter, we will first like give you a brief account of our organization, which has been at the forefront in the struggle to protect Fako lands that are now threatened by the privatization of the CDC. Fako elements in the United States who now number well over 1000 (one thousand), and who have been closely following the CDC privatization debates since 1994, decided to form a branch of the Bakweri Land Claims Committee. The aim was to give them an opportunity to actively join the struggle for the restoration of our rights on our ancestral lands. For reasons of good order, Fako elements in the Diaspora supported the move by the home branch to reorganize itself into a properly constituted entity with an identifiable and democratically elected leadership structure. It was our belief that such an entity would be best placed to effectively handle any negotiations and discussions pertaining to the privatization of the CDC. Fako elements in the USA accordingly had the BLCC incorporated here in the USA as a non-profit body.

The principal objectives of the corporation, whose members are all of Fako origin, are:

to conduct activities which are charitable and educational . . . ; to educate and sensitize the public on BLCC's efforts to reclaim expropriated ancestral lands; to encourage wise and rational development of these lands; to interest young Bakweri men and women in the Diaspora to join together to exploit these lands for the betterment of their people; and to these ends, organize fund-raising events, solicit and apply for private and public grants.

Among the restrictions enshrined in its Articles of incorporation are the following:

The corporation may not:

- Engage in activities or us its assets in a manner that do not further one or more exempt purposes . . .

- Serve as a private interest other than one clearly incidental to any overriding public interest.

- Devote more than an insubstantial part of its activities to attempting to influence legislation by propaganda or otherwise.

- Participate in or intervene in any political campaign on behalf of or in opposition to any candidate for public office. The prohibited activities include publishing or distributing statements and any other direct or indirect campaign activities.

- Distribute assets on dissolution other than for one or more exempt purposes.

- Permit any of the corporation's net earnings to inure to the benefit of any private individual.

- Carry on an unrelated trade or business, except a secondary purpose related to the Corporations primary exempt purposes.

> These objectives are to be implemented by a Board of Trustees, which comprises eminent Bakwerians and all Fako Chiefs (yourselves) who form the Chiefs Advisory Council.
>
> The interim Executive Bureau of the USA branch comprises:
> Dr. Lyombe Eko, Executive Director
> Dr. Njohi Endeley, Secretary General
> Mola Dibussi Tande, Director of Communications
> Dr. Emil Mondoa, Senior Adviser
> Iya Namondo Evakise, Fako America Representative.
>
> The BLCC as incorporated in America, is therefore a non-political and non— partisan corporation with a clearly non—profit agenda. It is an umbrella organization for all sons and daughters of Fako who are actively seeking justice with regards to expropriated indigenous lands in Fako.

As your excellencies are well aware, since 1994, the government of Cameroon has set in motion the process of privatizing the CDC whose agro-industrial facilities and activities occupy some 400 square miles of Bakweri land, with consulting the land owners or compensating them for past or present use.

The title to these lands was never vested in the CDC. It is well known and memorialized in countless legal instruments and official documents that the title to these lands never passed to the CDC, and that the Administering Authority, as well as the successor independent Cameroon Government, were merely acting as custodians, holding these lands in trust for present and future generations of Bakweri people. Indeed, the CDC itself recognized that it had only temporary use and occupation of the lands and made provisions in its book for annual payment of ground rents, which so far were wrongly paid to the public exchequer.

Since, 1946, the Bakweri Land Claims Committee has ear headed the struggle to have the lands returned to its rightful owners through petitions, demonstrations and representations in Cameroon and abroad.

More recently, the BLCC branch in the United States, BLCC-USA, and all the Fako elements around the world, have mounted a vigorous campaign on the Internet, at the United Nations, the international Monetary Fund (IMF) and the World Bank, to put the issue of Bakweri CDC lands on the international public agenda. Significant results have been achieved. These organizations have recognized the legality and validity of Bakweri claims under international human rights law. The international community has asked the Cameroon government to address the CDC land issue in the privatization.

After nearly a century of struggle by our people, spearheaded by the BLCC, things are moving in the right direction. However, in order than our hard fought, gains

are not be turned into ashes of defeat by some selfish individuals, we call on you, our leaders to do your part at
home while we fight abroad. All Bakweri chiefs and their
people must now stand firm, resolute and united in their
opposition to any attempt to disposes them once again
of these lands through legal manoeuvres assisted by self-
serving individuals in their own midst.

Indeed, the Fako elements around the world are ready to
repudiate and totally disown on radio, television, news-
papers and the Internet, each and every one of its leaders
who breaks ranks and makes it easy for our lands to be
lost. More than ever before, we believe that the actions
of all our chiefs should be guided by the interests and
wishes of our people, not their personal interests.

Your Excellencies, we assure you that if we fail to secure
our CDC lands because of the selfishness of a few, our
children and our children's children will never forgive us!
We the Fako elements in the United States of America
are confident that our chiefs do not want to be known
nationally or internationally as the traitors of their own
people or to go down in history as the ones who voted for
the enslavement and annihilation of their people.

Your Excellencies, We your children, wish once again
to underscore our position on the CDC privatization in
order that we speak with one unambiguous and united
voice. We would like you, our leaders, in cooperation
with the BLCC, to send a resolution to Government regarding compensation for the past and present use of our
land, as well as safeguards for the future.

Once again, we appeal to you to act as a united and
non-partisan force, and to team up to support the BLCC
which has already put forth comprehensive proposals to
the government on issues such as the rightful ownership
of CDC-occupied lands by the people of Fako; the privatization of the CDC and the payment of grounds rents to
the indigenous landowners; and the establishment of a

Cameroon-based Fako Trust Fund managed a Board of Trustees duly elected by the Fako people and their leaders, and whose mission will be to ensure that any benefits that may accrue shall be enjoyed by the people of Fako as a whole.

We entreat you to continue to support the BLCC in accomplishing the monumental and heroic struggle it has waged throughout the years and particularly at this critical period in the history of our people.

Please accept the renewed assurances of our highest esteem and consideration.

NAMONDO EVAKISE
President, Fako America
DR. LYOMBE EKO
Executive Director, BLCC-USA
DIBUSSI TANDE
Vice President, Fako America
Dr. NTOH ENDELEY
Secretary General, BLCC–USA
On behalf of the Fako Diaspora Community

Appendix 7

Letter of BLCC to the Managing Director of the IMF

[IMF Sanctioned Privatization of the Cameroon Development
Corporation . . .]Sanctioned Privatization of the Cameroon
Development Corporation
Challenged
Robert Weissman
Tue, 27 Jun 2000 10:12.32-0400 (EDT)
BAKWERI LAND CLAIMS COMMITTEE-USA
P.0. Box 433,
Orono, ME, 04473-9998
U.S.A
Fax: (425) 955-9218
Email: Web: http: /
Mr. Horst Koehler Managing Director International
Monetary
Fund
700 19th Street, N.W.
Washington, D.C. 20431
June 16, 2000

Dear Mr. Managing Director:

Subject: IMF SANCTIONED PRIVATIZATION of CAMEROON DEVELOPMENT CORPORATION (CDC), WITHOUT CONSULTATION WITH THE NATIVE LANDOWNERS.

We, the Bureau of the Bakweri Land Claims Committee—USA (BLCC-USA), together with our fellow Fako indigenes living in all continents of the world, assembled through the revolutionary technology of the Internet, have been made to understand that in June 2000, the IMF Board of Directors reviewed the Enhanced Structural Adjustment Facility (ESAF)/ Poverty Reduction and Growth Facility (PRGF) program of the Republic of Cameroon, and that the Managing Director, Mr. Horst Koehler, will be visiting Cameroon in July 2000. The country's privatization scheme is being carried out under this program. Cameroon government—controlled parastatal companies scheduled to be privatized under the ESAF/PRGF program include the Cameroon Development Corporation (CDC), an agro—industrial company located mainly in Fako Division, home of the indigenous Bakweri people.

The Bakweri, speaking through the Bakweri Land Claims Committee in the U.S.A. (BLCC-USA) hereby reiterate their unwavering opposition to any privatization program that does not take into consideration the legitimate rights of the natives whose ancestral lands the soon to be privatized CDC and its colonial predecessors, have exploited without compensation for more than a century.

We wish to state that more than 380 square miles of land currently occupied by the CDC, virtually all of Fako division's most fertile land, were forcefully and brutally expropriated from our forefathers without compensation, by German colonizers in the late l9th century for purposes of large—scale plantation agriculture. In 1947, these plantations were leased to the CDC by the British colonial government which had seized them from the Germans after World War II, on terms that they would be held in trust for the indigenous native Bakweri until such time that they were able to manage the plantations themselves. In 1960 the British colonial administration ceded power to the Government of Southern Cameroons, which has now been succeeded by the Government of the Republic of Cameroon.

Under the terms of the lease of these lands to CDC, the latter was required to pay annual ground rent, for the benefit of the disposed indigenous natives. The native Bakweri have never been paid any part of these rents, and with privatization looming in the horizon, whereby their lands will be alienated the foreign companies, the Bakweri resolutely refuse to recognize any privatization of the CDC that does not take into account the just, long—standing and legitimate rights of the Bakweri over their land. (Please see United Nations Trusteeship Agreements of 1946 and 1947, and the 1960 Land Lease Agreement at the BLCC—USA website:

The position of the Bakweri, the land owners, is that while they are not opposed to privatization per se, the rental terms under which their land is leased to foreign developers should be clearly spelt out and acceptable to them, with a clear statement of the reversionary Bakweri interest in the land.

It must also be pointed out that since this region is the habitat et many endangered wildlife species including mountain gorillas, antelopes and elephants, prospective lessees of lands currently occupied by the CDC should also be made aware of their obligations within the framework of internationally recognized environmental norms. The terms of privatization should be clearly spelt out and should recognize the ownership of land as a distinct variable which, together with capital and labor, makes plantation agriculture possible.

The BLCC position is consistent with the Universal Declaration of Human Rights, and Article 21 of the African

Charter of Human and Peoples' Rights of 1981 which states, inter alia:

"1. All peoples shall freely dispose of their wealth and natural resources. This right shall be exercised in the exclusive interest of the people. In no case shah a people be deprived of it.

2. In case of spoliation, the dispossessed people shall have the right to the lawful recovery of its property as well as to an adequate compensation."

As the current impasse in Zimbabwe and Kenya demonstrate, land expropriated from African natives by European colonialists a century age is the source of much contemporary unrest and instability. All Cameroonians of goodwill bear witness that the Bakweri people have over the years opted for a peaceful resolution of this CDC Bakweri land problem. However should the privatization of the CDC go ahead without the input of the Bakweri on whose land most of the corporation's agro-industrial activities are located, we reserve the right to seek legal redress against the Government et the Republic of Cameroon, the IMF, the World Bank as well as all lessees who derive title to the land by whatever means, in any country et the world where such bodies are located.

In furtherance of the above stated objective, the BLCC-USA will associate with the international mass media, environmental groups, Human Right groups and other non-governmental organizations around the world, in its just struggle against exploitation of ancestral lands without compensation to the dispossessed landowners.

It is worthy of note to all concerned with the privatization of the CDC that there is right now very high socio—political tension in the English—speaking provinces of Cameroon, where the lands under discussion are to be found. Privatizing the CDC without the consent and participation of the native landowners carries grave risks especially to potential investors, as the object lesson in Zimbabwe and Kenya amply illustrates.

The world must learn to prevent conflicts, as the cost of putting them out is usually disproportionately high, in terms of human lives and resources.

BLCC-USA sincerely hopes that its timely appeals will be headed to, in the interest of equity, peace, and national unity of present and future generations of Cameroonians.

Please accept the expression of our highest esteem.

For and on behalf of BLCC-USA and the Bakweri around the world.

Lyombe Eko, Ph.D. Executive Director, BLCC-USA

Njoh Endeley, Ph.D.
Secretary General, BLCC-USA

Dibussi Tande
Director of Communications, BLCC-USA

Emil Mondoa, M.D.
Senior Adviser-BLCC-USA

Jack Endeley
President, Fako America

cc
The President
The World Bank Group
1818 H Street, N.W. Washington, DC 20433

Mr. Serge Michailof
Country Director, Cameroon
Room # J 7-157
1818 H Street, N.W. Washington D.C. 20433

Mr. Robert Lacey
Cameroon Resident Representative
World Bank Field Office
Street 1.792, No. 186
New Bastos, Po Box 1128
Yaounde, Cameroon

Bon. Jesse Helms,

Chairman, Foreign Relations Committee
United States Senate
Washington DC

Hon. Edward R. Royce
Chairman of the U.S. Congress Subcommittee on Africa
H I—705 O'Neill House Office Building
Washington, DC 20515

The Honorable Susan E. Rice
Assistant Secretary of State for African Affairs
U.S. Department of State
Washington, D.C. 20520

Ambassador Jerome Mendouga
Embassy of the Republic of Cameroon
2349 Massachusetts Avenue, NW Washington DC, 20008

Appendix 8

BLCC Pilgrimage to Dakar in May 2004

BAKWERI LAND CLAIMS COMMITTEE
(Incorporated;
Registered as 01 in the Companies Registering,
Limbe)
PO. BOX 124
BUEA CAMEROON
Email:
22nd February, 2004 Tel/Fax: 332 22 02; Mobile: 950
77 09: email:

Dear Mola/lya

BLCC Pilgrimage to Dakar in May 2004

Ever Since the BLCC started its international campaign for the restoration of Bakweri ancestral land rights before the judicial panel of the African Commission on Human & Peoples' Rights, two important delegations were dispatched last year to plead the BLCC case before the African Commission.

The first delegation of five travelled to Niamey, Republic of Niger, where BLCC was awarded an Injunction against the Government of Cameroon, restraining it from further alienation of CDC disputed lands, until the matter before the Commission is finally determined. The African Commission clearly understood the gravity of the Bakweri complaint. On retuning to Cameroon, the BLCC again pleaded with the Government to initiate negotiations for an amicable settlement of the dispute, but there has been no reaction, as hitherto, to this request. The second delegation of six persons went to Banjul, the Gambia, only last November, where both parties to the dispute made oral presentations in support of their respective written pleadings. As the BLCC matter has caught the eye of the International community, the University of Tennessee, USA, sent to Banjul an attorney from its legal clinic, to lend support to BLCC's lead counsel 's submissions.

The Court deferred delivering a decision on the Admissibility of the BLCC complain to its next Session in Dakar, Senegal, in May 2004. Barring the unpredictable, BLCC fuels reasonably confident that the Commission will declare the complaint admissible, in spite of Respondent's abortive attempts to intimidate the leadership of the BLCC by subjecting it to frivolous criminal investigations, and with the connivance of the Fako High Court.

The cost of the return air fares, plus hotel and incidental expenses, has averaged circa 1.2 million FRS per delegate, and I would like to express my deep appreciation to all those who have contributed in sustaining the struggle thus far. The trip to Dakar is vital, and I wish to invite you all, especially those, who have not yet made contribution to the struggle for Bakweri prosperity, to now demonstrate allegiance to the fatherland.

This is a pre-alert, for a BLCC delegation shall be calling on you before the end of April to receive your generous support for this worthy cause which transcends party politics.

A Njoh Litumbe
Secretary-General

Appendix 9

Letter of BLCC to the Managing Director of the IMF (French version)

M. le Directeur Général
Fonds monétaire international
700 19th Street, N.W. Washington, DC 20431 USA
Monsieur le Directeur Général.
Objet :
PRIVATISATION DE LA CAMEROON
DEVELOPMENT
CORPORATION
(CDC)
CAUTIONNEE PAR LE FMI, SANS
CONSULTATION
AVEC LES
PROPRIETAIRES AUTOCHTONES DES
TERRES

Nous, membres du Bureau exécutif du Comité des revendications foncières des Bakweri aux Etats-Unis Q3LCC-USA), en collaboration avec les indigènes du Fako habitant dans tous les continents du monde, rassemblés par la technologie révolutionnaire d'Internet, avons pris connaissance du fait que, au mois de juin

2000, le Conseil d'administration du FMI s'est mis à réexaminer le programme de la facilité d'ajustement structurel renforcé (FASR)/ facilité pour la réduction de la pauvreté et la croissance (FRPC) pour la République du Cameroun, et que le Directeur Général. M. Horst Köhler, se rendra au Cameroun au mois de juillet 2000. La campagne de privatisation du pays se poursuit dans le cadre de ce programme. Parmi les entreprises de l'Etat gérées par le gouvernement camerounais et destinées à être privatisées sous les auspices du programme FASR/FRPC, se trouve la Cameroon Development Corporation (CDC), une société agro-industrielle située principalement dans le Département du Fako, demeure du peuple indigène Bakweri.

Le peuple Bakweri, par l'intermédiaire du Comité des revendications foncières des Bakweri aux Etats-Unis d'Amérique (BLCC-USA), réitère par la présente son inconditionnelle opposition à tout programme de privatisation qui ne tient pas compte des droits légitimes des peuples autochtones dont les terres ancestrales sont exploitées sans aucune indemnisation depuis plus d'un siècle par la future société privée, la Cameroon Development Corporation(CDC) et par ses prédécesseurs coloniaux.

Nous aimerions indiquer que plus de 988 kilomètres carrés de terres actuellement occupées par la CDC, soit pratiquement toutes les terres les plus fertiles du Département du Fako, furent violemment et brutalement arrachés à nos ancêtres sans indemnisation, par le colon allemand vers la fin du 19e siècle, dans le but d'établir des plantations agricoles de grande envergure. En 1947, ces plantations furent louées à la CDC par l'administration coloniale britannique, laquelle les avait saisies aux mains des Allemands à la fin de la première guerre mondiale et était supposée les tenir en tutelle au nom des indigènes Bakweri jusqu'à ce que ces derniers furent capables de les gérer eux-mêmes. En 1960, l'administration coloniale britannique céda le pouvoir au Gouvernement du Cameroun Méridional, lequel a succédé par le Gouvernement de la République du Cameroun.

Selon les termes de la location de ces terres à la CDC, cette dernière est tenue de verser un loyer en faveur des indigènes dépossédés. Les autochtones Bakweri n'ont jamais Les autochtones Bakweri n'ont jamais perçu aucune indemnisation et au fur et à mesure que s'approche la privatisation qui donnerait leurs terres à des sociétés étrangères, les Bakweri refusent résolument de reconnaître toute privatisation de la CDC qui ne tient pas compte de leurs droits de propriété justes, légitimes et de longue durée sur leur terre. (Veuillez consulter les Accords de Tutelle des Nations Unies de 1946 et 1947) ainsi que l'Accord de location foncière de 1960 et autres documents au site web du BLCC-USA: www. bakwerilands. org

Les Bakweri, les propriétaires de ces terres, ne sont pas contre la privatisation en tant que tel. Cependant, ils voudraient que les termes de la location de leurs terres à des exploiteurs étrangers soient clairement établis, que ces termes leur soient acceptables et qu'il y ait une claire indication de leur droit fondamental à ces terres.

Il faut également noter que, puisque cette région est la demeure de plusieurs espèces en danger d'extinction, y compris le gorille, l'antilope et l'éléphant, les potentiels acheteurs ou locataires des terres actuellement occupées par la CDC devront prendre connaissance de leurs obligations dans le cadre de normes écologiques reconnues par la communauté internationale. Les termes de la privatisation devront être clairement indiqués et devront reconnaître la propriété foncière comme une variable distincte qui, en collaboration avec le capital et la main

d'œuvre, rend l'agriculture de plantation possible.

La position prise par le BLCC est en conformité avec la Déclaration universelle des droits de l'homme, ainsi qu'avec l'article 21 de la Charte africaine des droits humains et des peuples de 1981, laquelle stipule, entre autres:

1. Tous les peuples auront le droit de disposer librement de leurs richesses et ressources naturelles. Ce droit sera exercé dans l'intérêt exclusif du peuple. En aucun cas le peuple n'en sera privé.

2. En cas de spoliation, le peuple dépossédé aura le droit à la récupération légale de sa propriété ainsi qu'à une indemnisation adéquate.

Tel que le démontre l'actuelle impasse au Zimbabwe et au Kenya, la terre arrachée aux autochtones africains par les colons européens depuis un siècle constitue aujourd'hui la source de beaucoup de bouleversements et d'instabilité. Tous les Camerounais de bonne foi sont témoins au fait que le peuple Bakweri a opté pour une solution pacifique au problème foncier de la CDC. Cependant, si la privatisation de la CDC se poursuit sans la participation des Bakweri dont les terres abritent la plupart des activités agro-industrielles de la société, nous nous réservons le droit de rechercher le recours juridique contre le Gouvernement de la

République du Cameroun, le FMI, la Banque mondiale ainsi que tous les locataires détenant des titres fonciers à ces terres par quelque moyen que ce soit, dans tout pays du monde où se trouverait un tel organisme.

Dans la poursuite de l'objectif cité ci-dessus, le BLCC-USA se propose de s'associer avec les médias internationaux, les groupes écologiques, les groupes des droits humains et autres organisations non gouvernementales de par le monde. Cela dans le cadre de sa lutte contre l'exploitation des terres ancestrales sans indemniser les propriétaires dépossédés.

Il est porté à l'attention de toutes les parties impliquées dans la privatisation de la CDC qu'il existe actuellement un niveau de tension socio-politique très élevé dans les provinces anglophones du Cameroun, la région où sont situées les terres en question. Privatiser la CDC sans le consentement ni la participation des propriétaires autochtones des terres constitue un grand danger surtout à l'égard de potentiels investisseurs, comme l'a abondamment illustré la leçon du Zimbabwe et du Kenya. Le monde doit apprendre à prévenir les conflits car le coût de les éteindre est souvent disproportionné en termes de vies humaines et de ressources.

Le BLCC-USA espère sincèrement que son appel sera entendu dans l'intérêt de l'équité, la paix, et l'unité nationale des générations futures de Camerounais.

Veuillez agréer, monsieur le directeur, l'expression de nos sentiments les plus distingués.

Au nom du BLCC-USA et des Bakweri de par le monde.

Signataires: Lyombe Eko, Ph.D.
Directeur Exécutif du BLCC-USA
Njoh Endeley, Ph.D.
Secrétaire-Général du BLCC-USA
Dibussi Tande
Directeur de Communication du BLCC-USA
Emil Mondoa, M.D.
Conseiller Principal du BLCC-USA
Jack Endeley
Le Président de l'association Fako America

Appendix 10

Crisis in the CTE (French Embassy)

French EMBASSY IN CAMEROON
ECONOMIC MISSION   Editor: RJ
Reviewed by:
06/04/2003

Crisis of Cameroon Tea Estate

The privatization of the CDC tea sector

Before giving 65% of its shares in the tea sector to the consortium Cameroon Tea Estates, the State was the sole shareholder of the CDC, Concession of 98,000 ha, of which 41,000 were highlighted for the cultivation of hevea, palm oil, banana and tea.

Under pressure from the IMF and the WB, CDC privatization process began in spring 1999 with call for pre-qualification, followed in September 2000 with the launching of the first call for tender. The government opted for privatization by "department", providing for the transfer of the majority of each sector to a strategic partner / shareholder (this does not exclude the possibility of tendering for more sectors).

The first call for tender not being successful, a new pre-qualification was launched in February 2001, after which Sofica (Fruiterer Co.), Del Monte, Agrisol, Michelin,

Cameroon Tea Estates and Socfinco were selected. The two main potential buyers, Fruiterer Co. (Fr) and Del Monte (US) interested in a global offer did not bid in the second tender (tender submission in July 2001).

Finally, in May 2002, the National Cameroon Tea Estates consortium was declared provisional contractor of the "tea" sector. The State sold 65% of its shares to a consortium led by the South African company Brobon Finex PTY Limited on 18th October. Cameroon Tea Estates pledged to increase production to 500 ha over 5 years on Ndu, Tole and Djutitsa production sites, to achieve an investment programme worth more than 12 million EUR over 10 years, and repay the debt of 1.6 million EUR committed to the sector. According to the government policy on privatization of agro-industries, land, placed under very long lease, remained State property and are. The twists of the case of Niba Ngu

Mid-January, the Cameroonian press widely reported the throes of privatization, following the sacking of the manager of the Cameroon Tea Estates from his position as operations manager. Daily Changes headline in an article of January 14th "the South African buyer would be a shell company."

The newspaper claims that Mr Niba Ngu, former GM of CDC, former Minister of Agriculture and former GM of SOCAPALM long interested in the resumption of the tea sector would have shared to Alhadji Baba Ahmadou Danpoullo of this interest and his need to find a financial partner.

The South African company Brobon Finex would be back in touch with former minister shortly after, these steps leading to the signing of a joint venture agreement creating the Cameroon Tea Estates. One of the strong terms of the partnership signed African partner by Chris Faraday, and Derrick G. Garvie (respectively Board Chairman and GM of Brobon Finex) was the designation of "John Niba Ngu as GM of CTE for a period of 10 years under conditions to be specified later ".

The newspaper reports that on October 19th, 24 hours after the signing of the agreement session, Baba Ahmadou he himself as Board Chairman of Brobon Finex and taking important managerial decisions: appointing 23 higher staffs with Deputy General Manager, Mr. Mahamat Alamine Mey. A few days later, he sells in advance the annual tea production at 2.2 billion FCFA, transferred to an account of CTE domiciled in Credit Lyonnais. 446 million FCFA are debited the following month and 2 billion transferred 10 days later in an account belonging to Cameroon TL.

The dismissal of the GM of CTE comes after his attempt to dismiss his deputy, and the other 22 newly recruited higher staffs, under the pretext that they were imposed illegally and knew nothing of tea.

The Brobon Finex board of January 4th (chaired by Ahmadou Baba) confirmed this unanimous decision and appoints the Deputy Director for the interim. Whereas the decisions taken during the board meeting of Brobon did not bound in any way CTE. Mr Niba Ngu commenced proceedings before the High Court of Fako, after which he was relocated briefly to general management (decision of justice Mbua A. Assanga of 8th January 2003).

The case bounced to January 10th, the Attorney General of the South West Court of Appeal signing a decision ordering until further notice the suspension of the services of Mr. Niba Ngu as GM.

The anglophone press has largely passed the stages of this managerial crisis (<Court reinstates Niba Ngu as GM but Attorney General says no! "In The Herald of 14/0l/03); Bakweri claims (" La colère du Sud-ouest" highlighted by Le Messenger of 18/01/03; "Bakweri landowners

threaten to sue buyers in South Africa" on the cover page of the Herald of 8/01/03).

For the essential, members of the BLCC (Bakweri Land Claim Committee) challenge a transfer that was made without the question of the devolution of land being resolved. They believe that "the rights of native Bakweri on the lands of Tole/Bwiyuku are intangible" and warned, through correspondence, the Executive Chairman of Brobon Finex, Derrick C. Garvie against "misrepresentation" of the Minister of Finance and Budget Michel Meva'a Meboutou who supported in Cameroon Tribune, a day after the signing of the transfer agreement with Brobon Finex for the tea sector, that the land occupied by tea plantations are "State property."

BLCC, claiming to have been side-lined for privatization which was not been done transparently addressed a letter to the government asking it to annul the privatization (Bakweri tell government to revoke privatization of CDC tea estates " highlighted in the Herald of January 22-23).

Following the request of the Presidency to investigate the disputed purchase of Tole, Ndu and Djutitsa plantations("Biya orders Musonge to investigate scandal on sale of CDC tea estates ", 21-23 February 2003), more issues are raised in the press (minister of Finance says Brobon tricked government "Herald of 21-23 march 2003).

- The purchase price of the CDC, which would have been sold off 1.5 billion FCFA, while the experts evaluated at 3,191,000,000 FCFA

- The questionable source of funds

- The unresolved issue of management, with the figure of Baba Ahmadou at the backdrop

- The questionable legal status of the majority shareholder Brobon Finex.

Regional Economic Mission: Cameroon, Chad,
Central African Republic, Equatorial Guinea
P. O. Box: 102–Plateau Atemengue–Yaounde
Tel. (237) 222 79 70–Fax: (237) 222 79 79.
E-mail: yaounde@dree.org
Website: http://www.dree.org.cameroun

Appendix 11

CTE in question (French Embassy)

17/04/03
FRENCH EMBASSY IN CAMEROON
ECONOMIC MISSION
Editor:
Reviewed by:
Note on the privatization of the CDC "tea" sector

Reminder on the privatization process

Before giving 65% of its shares in the "tea" sector of the Cameroon Development Corporation to the Cameroon Tea Estates consortium, the State was the sole shareholder of CDC, concession 98,000 hectares of which 41,000 were highlighted for the cultivation of hevea, palm oil, banana and tea.

Under pressure from the IMF and the WB, CDC privatization process began in spring 1999 by call for pre-qualification, followed in September 2000 with the launching of the first call for tender. The government opted for privatization "by sector", with the transfer of the majority of each to a strategic partner/shareholder (this does not exclude the possibility of tendering for more than one).

The first call for tender not being successful, a new pre-qualification was launched in February 2001, after which Sofica (Fruiterer Co.), Del Monte, Agrisol, Michelin, Cameroon Tea Estates and Socfinco were selected. The two main potential buyers, the Fruiterer Co. (Fr) and Del Monte (US) interested in a total package, should not bid in the second call for tender (tender submission in July 2001).

Finally, in May 2002, the Cameroon Tea Estates consortium was declared provisional contractor of the "tea" sector and the State thus gave in 65% of her shares on 18th October. Cameroon Tea Estates pledged to increase production of 500 ha over 5 years on Ndu, Tole and Djutitsa production sites, to realize an investment programme worth more than 12 million EUR over 10 years, and to repay a debt of 1.6 million EUR attached to the sector. According to government policy on privatization of agro-industries, land, put under very long lease, should remain State property.

Dissensions within the C.T.E

The Cameroon Tea Estates joint venture consortium created for the occasion between the South African company Brobon Finex and a former agriculture minister of Cameroon, Mr Niba Ngu, was represented at the tender negotiations by Mr Chris Faraday and Mr Derrick G . Garvie, respectively Board Chairman and Operations Manager of Brobon Finex. It was also understood that, according to an agreement between Brobon Finex and her Cameroonian partner, the latter was appointed as GM of consortium for a period of 10 years under conditions to be specified later.

But the day after the transfer of shares of the State to the CTE, a new partner of the South African group appeared in the person of Mr. Alhaji Baba Ahmadou Danpoullo, a Cameroonian business man well known in the place and

already involved in a financial package challenged during a privatization project of SODECOTON. This new
manager, previously hidden, then proceeded to appoint
a new management team (twenty higher staffs) under
the leadership of a DGM, also coming from outside, Mr.
Mahamat Alamine Mey.

Mr Niba Ngu having opposed the appointments in his
capacity as GM, and having decided to dismiss all the
newcomers, was then sacked, which led him to initiate
legal action to be reinstated into his rights. A succession
of conflicting decisions and appeal ended on January
10th at the Court of Appeal, by the confirmation of the
suspension of Mr. Niba Ngu from his duties as GM.

Comments

Although at this stage the matter appears settled, a number of challenging elements have not been clarified and
are controversial which the press is still echoing and
concern:

The purchase price by C.T.E. of the 65% held by the State;

The exact nature of the business and reputation of Brobon Finex, filthy company likely to mobilize funds of
dubious origin or mare name-giving of Cameroonian
interests;

The bi or tri-headed management of a new corporation
of which the first decision of sales of its annual production has made obvious the effect of questionings;

The exact rate, in the mounting operation of the CDC /
CTE, of Cameroonian personalities with unconventional
career or with a past somewhat sulphurous;

The question of the devolution of land concerned by the transfer to CTE mentioned by the Minister of Finance in his terms challenged by Bakweri Land Claim Committee;

The legal mess that results from ongoing litigation.

In short, it seems arguable that this privatization took place once again in less orthodox and in obscure conditions, otherwise unhealthy, which may jeopardize the future of the company, which again pose the question of good governance of Cameroon's economy and which confirm that transparency is obviously a prerequisite for the success of such operations.

Regional Economic Mission: Cameroon, Chad, Central African Republic, Equatorial Guinea
P. O. Box: 102-Plateau Atemengue-Yaounde
Tel. : (237) 222 79 70-Fax (237) 222 79 79
Email: yaounde@dree.org
Website: http://www.dree.org.cameroun

Appendix 12

Map of Mount Cameroon

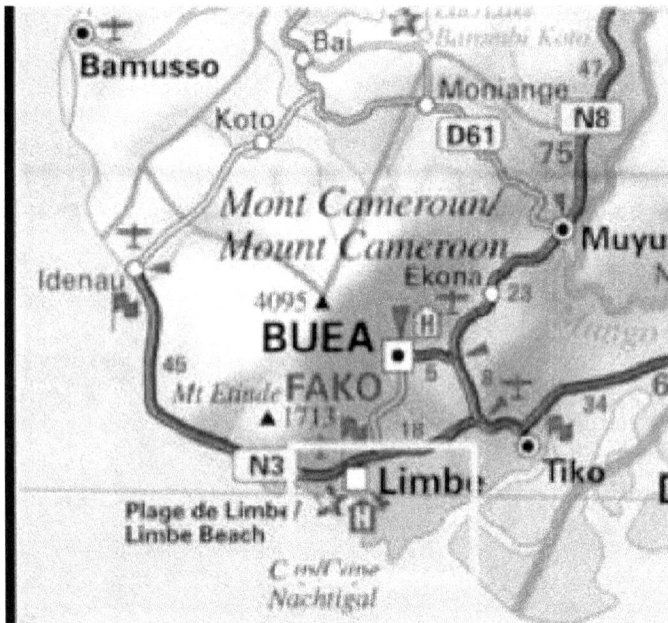

Appendix 13

Authorization of the CDC

CAMEROON DEVELOPMENT CORPORATION

(Incorporated under Decree No. 082/38 of 22 January 1982)

Development Company with Capital in share 15,626,328,000 F.CFA

TELEPHONE LIMBE: 3431883
BOTA-LIMBE, FAKO DIVISION
TELEX LIMBE : 5242KN
SOUTH WEST PROVINCE
CABLES: "DEVCAM"
LIMBE, CAMEROON
FAX 343 1746
REPUBLIC OF CAMEROON
343 18 76
30 March 2005
DHR/AD/2
TMS/AD/2
Kibangou Hermann-Habib,
Catholic University of C.A.
Faculty of Science &
Management, Nkolbisson Campus, Yaounde.

Dear Sir.

APPLICATION TO CARRY OUT RESEARCH

I refer to your letter dated 23rd March, 2005 on the above subject and write to inform you that your request has been granted.

You will report to the Manager, Human Resources Development Service (MHRDS) Head Office Bota who by copy of this letter is requested to assist you by providing the necessary information for your research study with effect from 4th April to 4th May 2005.

You will have the obligation to submit a copy of your final report to the Training Manager for the Corporation's library.

You should show proof that you are covered by a third party insurance policy for damage that you may cause to Corporation property.

cc IMHRDS/MTMS

Appendix 14

Organigram of the CDC

CDC-Charter of Management-1996

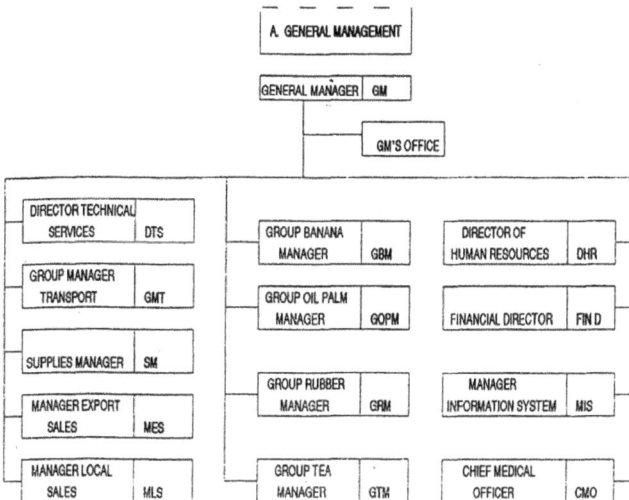

A. GENERAL MANAGEMENT	

GENERAL MANAGER	GM

GM'S OFFICE

DIRECTOR TECHNICAL SERVICES	DTS
GROUP MANAGER TRANSPORT	GMT
SUPPLIES MANAGER	SM
MANAGER EXPORT SALES	MES
MANAGER LOCAL SALES	MLS

GROUP BANANA MANAGER	GBM
GROUP OIL PALM MANAGER	GOPM
GROUP RUBBER MANAGER	GRM
GROUP TEA MANAGER	GTM

DIRECTOR OF HUMAN RESOURCES	DHR
FINANCIAL DIRECTOR	FIN D
MANAGER INFORMATION SYSTEM	MIS
CHIEF MEDICAL OFFICER	CMO

Bibliography

Abdoul Bagui, Kari. Regard sur les privatisations au Cameroun : suivi d'un recueil de textes, CEMAC, [Cameroun ? s.n.], 2001.

Abega, Sévérin-Cécile, *Cultures des peuples d'Afrique centrale*. Notes de cours, UCAC, 2003–2004.

Aerts, Jean-Joël, Cogneau, Denis, Herrerra, Javier, de Monchy, Guy, Roubaud, François, *L'économie camerounaise. Un espoir évanoui*, Paris, Karthala, 2000.

Amin, Samir, *L'accumulation à l'échelle mondiale*, Paris, Anthropos, 1988.

———. 1995. Mondialisations et particularismes. Les conditions d'une relance du développement », CIFEDHOP collection thématique, Paris, CIFEDHOP, 1995, pp.9–31.

Ayuk, A. Kima Prince et Lyonga, Matute Daniel, *Introducing Limbe*, Limbe, Presbyterian Printing, 1990.

Azebaze, Alex Gustave. 2003. Le pouvoir intimide les Bakweri. In Le Messager n° 1526 du lundi 23 juin 2003, p.4.

———. 2003. Suspension possible de la privatisation de la Cdc », in Le Messager n° 1526 du lundi 23 juin 2003, p.4.

Baecheler , Jean, *Qu'est-ce que l'idéologie ?* Paris, Gallimard, 1976.

Banque mondiale, *L'Afrique sub-saharienne, de la crise à une croissance durable*, Washington, Banque mondiale, 1989.

Barre, Raymond, *Économie politique*, Paris, P.U.F. (8è éd. refondue), 1969.

Bayart, Jean-François, *L'État en Afrique. La politique du ventre*, Paris, Fayard, 1989.

Beaud, Michel, *L'art de la thèse*, Paris, éditions La Découverte, 1990.

Bederman, Sanford H., *The Cameroons Development Corporation; partner in national growth*, Bota, West Cameroon: Cameroons Development Corporation, 1968.

Bekolo-Ebe Bruno, Touna, Mama, Fouda, Séraphin Magloire, *Dynamiques de développement. Débats théoriques et enjeux politiques à l'aube du 21è siècle. Mélanges en l'honneur de Georges Walter Ngango*. Collection Grands Colloques, Paris, Monchrestien, 2003.

Berger, Peter L., *Comprendre la sociologie*, Paris, Centurion, 1973.

Bernoux, Philippe, La *sociologie des organisations. Initiation*, Paris, Seuil, 1995.

Bizaguet, Armand, *Le secteur public et les privatisations,* Coll. Que sais-je ? Paris, PUF, 1988.

Bouin, Olivier, *La privatisation dans les pays en développement. Réflexion sur une panacée,* Paris, OCDE, 1992.

Calvez, Jean-Yves. 2001. Un siècle de lutte contre les inégalités du système capitaliste». In Croire Aujourd'hui n° 110, 1er avril 2001. Peut-on changer le capitalisme ? p.12.

Cameroon Development Corporation, *Annual report and accounts for the year ended 30th June 1999,* Limbe, Presbyterian Printing, 1999.

Chabal, Patrick et Daloz, Jean-Pascal, *L'Afrique est partie ! Du désordre comme instrument politique,* Paris, Economica, 1999.

Chavane, Bruno, « Bilan et perspectives des privatisations en Afrique francophone : une étape de la privatisation ? » Ed. O.I.T., Genève, 1998.

Colonial Develoment Corporation (CDC), *Report and accounts.* 1959. *Annual statement of accounts for the year to 31 December 1959, London,* 1959.

Crozier, Michel et Friedberg, Erhard, *L'acteur et le système,* Paris, Seuil, 1977.

Courade, Georges. 1981-1982. «Victoria Bota : croissance urbaine et immigration». In *Travaux et documents de l'ORSTOM.* Série Sciences Humaines. *Cahiers Orstom,* vol. XVIII, n° 3.

———. 1981-1982. Marginalité volontaire ou imposée? Le cas des Bakweri (KPE) du mont Cameroun ». In *Cahiers de l'ORSTOM.* Série Sciences Humaines, vol. XVIII, n° 3, 1981–1982: 357–388.

———. (sous la direction), *Le désarroi camerounais. L'épreuve de l'économie monde,* Paris, Karthala, 2000.

Demba,Thiam Papa, *Stratégies d'interface. Intégration économique et développement,* Berne, Ed. Peter Lang, 1991.

Diakite, Tidiane, *L'Afrique malade d'elle-même,* Paris, Karthala, 1986.

Durand Jean-Pierre and Robert Weil, Sociologie contemporaine, Paris, Vigot (2nd edit.), 1997.

Ela, Jean-Marc. 1999. Le rôle du savoir dans le développement agriculteurs et éleveurs au Nord-Cameroun. In Lisbet Holtedah, Siri Gerrard, Martin Z. Njeuma, Jean Boutrais (eds), *Le pouvoir du savoir de l'Arctique aux Tropiques,* Paris, Karthala.

Elias, Norbert, *Qu'est-ce que la sociologie ?* Paris, l'Aube, 1991.

Encyclopedie Economica, Paris, Economica, 1984.

Etounga–Manguele, Daniel, *L'Afrique a-t-elle besoin d'un programme d'ajustement culturel ?* Ivry-Sur-Seine, Ed. Nouvelles du Sud, 1991.

Jellal, Mohamed et François-Charles, Wolff. 2003. Privatisation et négociation collective ». In Revue d'Economie du Développement n° 1 mars 2003. Ed. de Boeck, p.73.

Gaud, Michel, *Les premières expériences de planification en Afrique noire,* Paris, Cujas, 1967.

Hamdouch, Abdelillah, *L'Etat d'influence. Nationalisations et privatisations en France,* Paris, Ed. Presses du CNRS, 1989.

Hastings, Michel, Aborder la science politique. Paris, Seuil, 1996.

Hebga, Meinrad Pierre, *Afrique de la foi. Afrique de la raison*, Paris, Karthala, 1995.

Gankou, Jean-Marie et Bondoma Yokono, Dieudonné. 2003. *Les privatisations dans le processus d'ajustement structurel au Cameroun* ». In Bruno Bekolo-Ebe, Touna, Mama, Fouda, Séraphin Magloire, *Dynamiques de développement. Débats théoriques et enjeux politiques à l'aube du 21è siècle. Mélanges en l'honneur de Georges Ngango*, Paris, Monchrestien, 287–293.

Giacobbi, Michèle Et Roux, Jean-Pierre, *Initiation à la sociologie*, Paris, Hatier, 1990.

Grawitz, Madeleine, *Lexique des sciences sociales*, Paris, Dalloz (7è éd.) ,2000.

Guillien Raymond et Vincent Jean, *Lexique des termes juridiques*, Paris, Dalloz (13è éd.), 2001.

Kamto, Maurice. 2003. *Tango juridique sur les privatisations au Cameroun*». In Bruno Bekolo-Ebe, Touna, Mama, Fouda, Séraphin Magloire, *Dynamiques de développement. Débats théoriques et enjeux politiques à l'aube du 21è siècle. Mélanges en l'honneur de Georges Ngango*, Paris, Monchrestien, 297–313.

Kibangou, Hermann-Habib. 2003. Rapport de stage effectué à la Cameroon Development Corporation (CDC) Bota-Limbé ». Du 1er juillet au 14 août 2003. UCAC 2002–2003.

Konings, Piet. 2003. *"Privatisation and ethno-regional protest in Cameroon"*. In *Afrika Spectrum* 38 (2003) 1: 5–26.

———. 2003. *"Mobility and exclusion: Conflicts between autochthons and allotochthons during political liberalisation in Cameroon"*. In Mirjam de Bruijn, Rijk Vaan Dijk, Dick Foeken (eds.), *Mobile Africa. Changing Patterns of Movement in Africa and beyond*, Leiden, Brill, 2003.

Enjangue, Théodore Et Noubissie Ngankam, *Les privatisations au Cameroun : bilan et perspectives*, Yaoundé, Fondation Friedrich Ebert, 1995.

Galal, Ahmed, Jones, Leroy, Tandon Pankaj, *Les effets de la cession d'entreprises publiques sur le bien-être général*, Washington, Banque mondiale, 1994.

Jacquemot, Pierre et Raffinot, Marc, *La nouvelle politique en Afrique noire*, VANVES, EDICEF, 1993.

Jeune Afrique Économie. *Hors Série. Cameroun cap sur l'an 2000*, Collection Marchés Nouveaux, août 1996.

Kabou, Axelle, *Et si l'Afrique refusait le développement ?* Paris, l'Harmattan, 1991.

Kamdem, Emmanuel, *Management et interculturalité en Afrique. Expérience camerounaise*, Québec/Paris, Ed. Les Presses de l'Université de Laval/ L'Harmattan 2002.

Kiamba, Claude-Ernest, *Politiques publiques*. Notes de cours, Yaoundé, UCAC, 2004–2005.

Lavigne Delville, Philippe, *Quelles politiques foncières pour l'Afrique rurale ? Réconcilier pratique, légitimité et légalité*, Paris, Karthala/Coopération française, 1998.

Le Bris (E.), Le Roy (E.), Leimdorfer (F.), *Enjeux fonciers en Afrique noire*, Ed. Paris, Orstom/Karthala, 1982.

Limbe Municipality, *The Limbe urban council magazine*, Third edition n°1 of September 2000.

Mebara Atangana, Jean-Marie, *La privatisation des monopoles de service public au Cameroun. Enjeux et évolution*, Yaoundé, Friedrich Ebert Liftung, 1997.

Lafaye, Dominique. 2003. La prise en compte de la dimension politique dans l'analyse économique». In Bruno Bekolo-Ebe et alii, 213.

Laïdi, Zaki, *Enquête sur la Banque mondiale*, Paris, Fayard, 1989.

Madelin, Henri, Le retour du politique». In *Etudes* janvier/2003, 5.

Mbembe, Achille, *Afriques indociles. Christianisme, pouvoir et État en société postcoloniale*, Paris, Karthala, 1988.

Medard, Jean-François (sous la direction de), *États d'Afrique. Formations, mécanismes et crise*, Paris, Karthala, 1991.

———. L'Etat patrimonialisé». In *Politique Africaine* n° 39, 11–12.

Melone, Stanislas, *La parenté et la terre dans la stratégie du développement. L'expérience camerounaise : étude critique*, Yaoundé/Paris, Université fédérale/Klincksieck, 1972.

Michalon, Thierry, *Quel État pour l'Afrique ?* Paris, L'Harmattan, 1984.

Monkam, André and Nzomo Joseph, Privatisations des entreprises publiques et para-publiques», in Conjoncture PME. La Revue Economique de l'Entreprise. Trimestriel d'informations, d'analyses et de prévisions économiques. N° 20—mars 2002/8è Année, 94.

Montousse, Marc Et Renouard, Gilles, *100 fiches pour comprendre la sociologie*, Paris, Ed. Bréal (5è éd.), 2001.

Mveng, Engelbert et Lipawing, Benjamin, *Théologie, libération et cultures africaines*, Ydé/Paris, Ed. Clé/Présence Africaine, 1995.

Ndeley Mokoso, Mola, Looking back from a child's eye». In Limbe municipality. The Limbe urban council magazine. Third edition n°1 of September 2000, 31–2.

Ngoupande, Jean-Paul, *Racines historiques et culturelles de la crise africaine*, Abidjan/Cotonou, Ad édit./éd. Du Pharaon, 1994.

Parys, Jean-Marie Van, *Petite introduction à l'éthique*, Kinshasa, Ed. Loyola, 1991.

Quivy, Raymond et Camperhoudt, Luc Van, *Manuel de recherche en sciences sociales*, Paris, Dunod (2è éd. entièrement revue et augmentée),1995.

République du Cameroun, *Régime foncier et domanial. Land tenure and state lands*, Yaoundé, Imprimerie nationale, 1974.

———. Décret n°86/656 du 03 juin 1986, article 2.

———. République du Cameroun, Ordonnance n°90/004 du 22 juin 1990, article 1er, alinéa 1.

Rocard, Michel, Le développement de l'Afrique, affaire de volonté politique »,
in Etudes janvier/2003, 21.

Rocher, Guy, Introduction à la sociologie générale. 1. L'action sociale, Ltée, HMH,
1968.

Rocher Joseph, Marchés (Avant-propos), in Rongead E. H., Série de 4 manuels
Marché local-marché national-marché international, vol. 1 Marchés,
novembre 1991, 53.

Sandouly, Patrick, Sur le papier et dans la rue ». In J.A./L'Intelligent n°2314 du
15 au 21 mai 2005, 55.

Savas, E.S., Privatisation. Partenariats public-privé, Paris, Nouveaux Horizons,
2000.

Smith, Stephen, Négrologie. Pourquoi l'Afrique se meurt, Paris, Ed. Calmann-
Lévy, 2003.

Soule, George, Qu'est-ce que l'économie politique ? Manille, Ed. Nouveaux
horizons, 1980.

Tevoedjre, Albert, La pauvreté, richesse des peuples, Paris, Ed. Économie et
Humanisme/Les éditions ouvrières, 1978.

Thomas, Joseph, Dialogue et vérité (Editorial), in Projet n°19, novembre 1967.
Civilisation, travail, économie. Ed. Imprimerie Saint-Paul, Paris, 1025.

Touraine, Alain, Comment sortir du libéralisme ? Paris, Fayard, 1999.

Toynbee, Arnold J., La civilisation à l'épreuve, Ed. Librairie Gallimard, Paris,
1951.

Valadier, Paul, Agir en politique. Décision morale et pluralisme politique, Ed. du
Cerf, Paris, 1980.

Weber, Max, Économie et société, Paris, Plon, 1971.

Wonyu, Emmanuel, Système économique mondial. Notes de cours, Yaoundé,
UCAC, 2003-2004.

Wright, Vincent (sous la direction), Les privatisations en Europe. Programmes et
problèmes, Poitiers, Ed. Actes du Sud, 1993.

www.bakwerilands.orgwww.ctpl.cm

www.banquemondiale.org

www.ctpl.cm/prog_en_cours/agro_in_CDC.htm

www.ctpl.cm/prog_en_cours/agro_in_coton.htm

www.limbecity.com

Zady Kessy, Marcel, Culture africaine et gestion de l'entreprise moderne, Ed.
CEDA, Abidjan, 1998.

www.ingramcontent.com/pod-product-compliance
Lightning Source LLC
Chambersburg PA
CBHW070921270326
41927CB00011B/2671